Find Your Spirit Animals

DAVID CARSON

Find Your Spirit Animals

Nurture, Guidance, Strength, and Healing from Your Inner Self

WATKINS PUBLISHING
LONDON

For Karen Douglas

Find Your Spirit Animals
David Carson

First published in the UK and the USA in 2011 by
Watkins Publishing
Sixth Floor, Castle House
75–76 Wells Street
London W1T 3QH

Conceived, created and designed by Watkins Publishing

Managing Editor: Sandra Rigby
Designer: Luana Gobbo
Commissioned artwork: Anna and Elena Balbusso, Lydia Hess

Library of Congress Cataloging-in-Publication Data available

ISBN: 978-1-78028-038-7

10 9 8 7 6 5 4 3 2 1

Typeset in Bell
Colour reproduction by Colourscan
Printed in China by Imago

Contents

INTRODUCTION

This book is about animals and how they are able to provide you with guidance and healing. Animal helpers or spirits are there for you to communicate with, to seek their assistance and direction. They can give you new abilities as well as refining abilities that you already have. The symbolism, legends and myths that surround each animal confirm their particular specialisms – those attributes that they can offer you. The bear, for example, is a great tracker and can help you find the things you desire. It is also a great warrior and can show you how to be brave and have courage to face life's battles. Besides having much practical knowledge to share, as do all the animals in this book, bear can also teach you about meditation and inner space.

Look to animals for naturalness, beauty and new ideas about how to live. Animals have an instinct for self-healing. They have enemies, of course, but they seek to live in harmony with their environment. They are realists and deal effectively with what is. Most can see, hear, taste, smell and possess tactile acuity beyond the powers of humans and we can learn much by tapping into their hyper-senses. The behavior of animals often speaks to our core values. Much like humans, animals highly value their lives but they are willing to sacrifice them to protect their young. Many examples of dedication and toil can be found in the animal kingdom. You need look no further than to the column of ants invading your next picnic to see their bravery, exactitude and work ethic.

Bond with the animal powers. As we move toward a life of advanced technology we forget the ancient, innate knowledge of the earth and of the animals. Yet this ancient wisdom is hardwired into our being, if we can only retrieve it. Honoring the animals can help us to remember our very humanity – and to perceive the web of life that connects all beings.

ANIMALS AND PEOPLE

Go back 150,000 years to a time when animals ruled the earth, and early man gazed out into the environment with fear and awe. He had different skill sets to animals. He did not have the claws or acute hearing and vision of the eagle; and he did not have a pointed beak or wings to fly like a bird. He was not fast like the gazelle, nor did he have menacing antlers; and he did not have the sharp teeth of the wolf. In fact, he had few defenses in very hostile surroundings, while living among creatures that had very powerful attributes and skills.

Perhaps one of our ancestors witnessed a saber-toothed tiger pounce on another animal and devour it, leaving its remains for the vultures. Cringing in terror and traumatized, this individual thought about the savage slaughter he had witnessed. He realized that animals had special talents and he began to pay close attention to them. The birds sang and made beautiful music, so he started to imitate their sounds and a power song was born: a song that took the singer's spirit on the wind so that it soared. He watched a butterfly flit about over flowers. Like the Cheyenne butterfly warriors, he learned how to dart and skip in the same manner to elude his enemy. He saw the flight of birds and knew that a large animal was approaching. As he watched, he realized that by imitating the animals he could learn the skills he needed in order to survive.

STORY FIRES

As long as there has been human history, people have gathered around campfires and told stories until the fire burned to embers. Story fires provided entertainment and helped people learn the tribal legends. They were the remembering fires, a place of warmth and sharing. Stories were told of daring feats, myths and, of course, they incorporated memories.

Ancient holy writ tells stories of peoples, prophets and angels – tales of our origins and of the cosmologies we live by. What kinds of stories influence your life? What is your character? And how have you been influenced by the stories you've read or heard?

We are all made from stories: stories of the past, stories of the future, our hopes and our dreams – once upon a time it happened. Think about your own story. Are you a tragedy, a comedy or a love story? Are you a tall tale or a boast? Perhaps you are a morality tale. Is your life poetic and your own mythology concealed within the stanzas and lyrics living within you, bringing you harmony and guidance on your path?

Take the time to reflect on your antagonists and the nature of the conflict in your personal story. Who are your friends and rivals? Consider your setting and your story's atmosphere. Do you want to change it? Here is your chance. Animals have their dramas too, in their lives and struggles. They figured prominently in the stories of the past – think of fairy tales by the Brothers Grimm, Hans Christian Andersen and the folk tales of every nation. Who does not remember stories of dangerous wolves in dark forests? There are humorous coyote stories; crow, rabbit and pig stories; stories of frog, bear and turtle, fox, goat and duck. Many animal tales are stories of survival where life and death are weighed in the balance. Animals have power struggles, battles for dominance in the pack and for the right to mate. Elephants grieve over death and return to smell and touch the bones of their dead herd members. The buffalo on the great plains could tell you a story of wanton killing and greed. And the eagle soars high and looks down on the animals and humans who are busy living their own stories.

THE WORLD OF THE SHAMAN

Enter the shaman. In tribal societies the shaman was an intermediary between people and the spirit world. He possessed special abilities to heal, to communicate and to guide through visionary experiences offering aid and clarity. His ritual garments protected him from evil spirits and were varied and flamboyant, exhibiting charms and other power objects. What is a shaman without a drum, without a song? Without singing and drumming there is no cohesion, no heart and no beauty or ceremony. Without power chanting there are no channels through which to enter the spirit realms – the territories of dreamers and mystics, the land beyond, where shamans go to make contact with other realities.

Every shamanic practice is underpinned by the presence of animals. Virtually every ancient culture revered animals and considered them to be of divine origin, creating rituals and methodology to contact animal spirits. These cultures believed that they could share in the strength and presence of the lion, the speed of the cheetah, the wisdom of the snake as well as the qualities of the owl, fox, eagle, wolf, bear and many other creatures. The animals, though often frightening, were also the catalyst for power and shamanic ability. No wonder there were so many animal dances and ritual celebrations of animal powers performed in the past. Humans realized that on a soul level there is a symbiotic relationship with animals; and if that relationship is broken, it is a great loss indeed.

Traditionally, shamans were the doctors, psychiatrists, storytellers and tribal philosophers who answered questions about the challenges and meaning of life. They were masters of energy and knew how to shift energy into positive configurations. They were often prophets who predicted the future, and their visions accurately told the best places to hunt and fish, and where certain medicinal and food plants were located.

Shamans move among three linked rings of existence. The first ring is our everyday experience or Normal Consciousness. The next ring is the Ring of Dreaming we access when we sleep. In dreams we can gain access to yet another dimension, the Ring of Death. It is believed we can pass into this ring and back again through a kind of cosmic revolving door. In the Ring of Death, shamanic cultures believe, we can be with the ancestors and can also find the master spirit of each animal. Dreams are also time machines because they have the power to take us back to the beginning or hurl us forward into the distant future. Such dream experiences are potent and holy, and rich with the possibility of acquiring shamanic abilities and powers. They can influence this journey that we call life in many positive ways. The shaman goes to spirit realms, bringing back power and knowledge that can be used in the Ring of Normal Consciousness.

THE DRUM

Shamans have, over the centuries, told of the "gift of horse" – the drum, which was often called the shaman's "horse". This drum horse could make the sound of galloping hooves and other mind-altering percussive beats. The striking of the drum is considered to be male, while the silence between the beats is female. The shaman rode this sound and was transported to other worlds where he would encounter animal spirits and other supernatural beings.

Each drum has its own vibration and resonance, and all shamanic drums are sacred. The drum is a circle of hide stretched and tied to a hollow wooden form. This form represents the universe, and because it is wooden, it unites us to the World Tree, the centering tree of life. The drum is circular and represents infinity, as well as the circle of the people. The ties symbolize the various clans who are tied together in a sacred manner. Usually, there is some artwork on the drum, its concept and design having been given to the owner in a dream or vision. Sometimes there are also metal disks, animal fetishes, tobacco ties or other objects fastened to the drum.

THE NATIVE AMERICAN EARTH WAY

Ten thousand books would not begin to tell the story of Native American shamanism, and perhaps the full account of shamanic belief and traditions can never be told. It is a rich and ancient story, going back to the hunting and gathering peoples of long ago.

Shamanism is the term commonly used today to describe the spiritual practitioners in Native North American cultures. The word, which was originally used to describe spiritual practices in Siberia, was imported by anthropologists and used to describe a wide range of indigenous traditions. Although the use of the term is controversial in some quarters, this book picks no quarrel with it.

Tribal peoples crisscrossed the back of Turtle Island, as the North American continent was known in pre-Colombian times (see page 50). No one knows for certain how many tribes there once were, but California alone had over 200. Many tribes died out and many others were absorbed into larger tribes. Despite war and persecution, today the spirit of the Native American wisdom lives on and is becoming more widely known and appreciated around the world.

Native American traditions differed among the many tribal groupings across North America but some key ideas seem to have been shared by all tribes. Perhaps the most important of these was the recognition that everything in the world was alive with spirit – the seasons, the plants, the earth, the sky and, of course, the animals. Humans were just one part of this great web of life, not superior to it.

In virtually all Native American myths and legends, animals play a key role helping and guiding humans. The importance of different animals reflected the environment in which the tribe lived. For the Dakota people of the Great Plains, the buffalo was crucial: a sacred bond existed between humans and buffalo, and the people's lives followed the movements of these great herds. For other tribes in the north, the bear was greatly admired for his courage and fearlessness.

The people of the Pacific Northwest carved totem poles that illustrated stories and animals associated with the group. They displayed the clan's heritage, which meant that a number of different animals could be shown. For example, the main clan might be an eagle with subclans such as beaver, fox, bear and frog. The symbols might record a memorable ceremony or a spiritual experience. Some animals might have offered the clan a special gift or shown the descent of the clan.

One concept found among many Native American tribes is that of the medicine wheel or sacred hoop. The wheel itself symbolizes the interconnectedness of life, and can represent the spiritual path we must take toward understanding. Medicine wheels were constructed from stones laid on the ground and could be used both for healing and ritual. Across the Americas the concept of the sacredness of the four cardinal directions is also very important. The precise symbolism varied between tribes. Among the Lakota, for example, each direction was represented by a different color – yellow for the east, white for the south, black for the west and red for the north. Each direction had its own particular energy.

SPIDER WOMAN

Spider Woman is one of the most important animals in Native American mythology. She plays a part in the traditions of several Native American tribes from modern-day Arizona, Utah and New Mexico, including the Navajo and the Hopi. She is generally associated with fertility and the beginnings of life, and provides assistance to people by teaching them survival skills.

THE REINDEER PEOPLE WAY

There are many lineages of Siberian shamanism – these peoples range from the northern tips of Scandinavia and Finland to Central Asia, Russia, Greenland, Alaska and northern Canada. Each tribe has distinctive elements to their shamanic practices. In the ancient tradition of Siberian shamanism in the Altai Mountains, where the mythical kingdom of Shambhala is reputed to be located, shamans travel through the dimensions of time and space. Using the drum and special breathing techniques, they can pass through various states of being and return safely from their visitations. Siberian shamans are said to possess a vital spirit – a power that has come down from the highest sky. This mysterious power sometimes manifests as an animal spirit, with the spirit ancestors appearing as a reindeer, a wolf, a bear or another animal. Shamans have diverse spirit helpers, including birds and fish.

In some Siberian shamanic practices, songs would be sung mimicking animals sounds – for example, among the Soyot people of Russia, singers would mimic the calls of birds and wolves who were seen as important spirit helpers. Among the Nganasan people, who live close to the Arctic Circle, shamans copy the sound of reindeer calves as this was believed to help women become fertile. Other shamans would sing the sound of the polar bear, and, in the process, it was thought that they could actually take on the spirit of the polar bear.

The reindeer people believed animals to have reincarnating souls and held that they must be properly respected. The bear was one the most important animals in Siberian cultures; for example, among the Mongolian peoples the word for bear was *baabgai,* related to the word for father, and there were elaborate ceremonies to honor a bear when one was killed. Among the pre-Christianized Finnish people, too, the bear was the most sacred animal.

He was seen as the embodiment of the ancestors and it was thought that his name must never be spoken aloud.

Birds were also very important in the Finnish tradition. They were believed to bestow a person's soul at birth and to take it away at death. In some cultures a wooden "soul-bird" or *sielulintu* was placed by a person's bed to protect their soul during sleep. Birds were also part of creation myths. Tradition held that the world was formed when a waterfowl's egg exploded, the sky being the upper half of the egg. At the very edge of the earth was the home of the birds, Lintukoto, while the Milky Way was considered the path the birds took on their journey there.

IS SANTA CLAUS A SHAMAN?

Santa is a transformational figure of the far northern lands of ice and snow associated with animals, which gives him shamanic overtones. Lapland, Siberia and Mongolia are the home of the reindeer people: herders who use reindeer not only for milk and other necessities but also as steeds – a specific echo of Santa Claus and his flying reindeer. Santa is old, wise and possesses mysterious powers that fit the profile of the shaman. He lives in the place of wisdom and spirit, and works to bring fairness through gift-giving. Just as the Siberian shamans call upon spirit helpers, Santa has elves. The Christmas tree, loosely associated with Santa, has an echo in northern European belief, for a cosmic tree sometimes links the different levels of the reindeer people's shared cosmology.

Santa's reindeer traditionally have bells around their necks. The shamans of the Finns and the Lapps often attached bells to their costumes to announce their presence in the Otherworld, as well as to warn off hostile spirits. The way of the reindeer people is the way of the drum, the heartsong way and the sacred way.

THE DREAMING WAY

Australia is an ancient land, and Aboriginal culture is said to be over 100,000 years old. The native people in Australia today are separated into more than 500 tribal groupings, and each group's oral history is an interweaving of story and song. With so many different tribal groupings spread across such a large continent, there is a wide range of mythic traditions and rituals, but many traditions have been lost post-European settlement. What we do know is that it's impossible to describe Aboriginal shamanism without reference to the "Dreaming" and the "Dreamtime". Aboriginal tradition holds that there are paths across the Australian landscape, known as the songlines or "dream tracks", and that these were created by the spirit ancestors who sang this world into being. Each traditional song is a length in the songline map.

The Dreamtime – a knit of ancestral legends, songs and stories – harks back to the time when ancestor spirits created plants and animals. In one tradition from eastern Australia, Baiame, an all-father creator god, came down from the sky in "the Dreaming" and created the lakes, rivers, forests, mountains and caves. He also brought song, tradition and law. When he was finished, his spirit lifted from the flattened Mount Yengo near the Wollombi Valley, north of Sydney, back into the spirit world from whence he came.

Dreaming stories are often attached to particular places. Some tell how Rainbow Serpent – a legendary being noted for the colorful, sparkling prism-like light that he casts – stirred and began to search Australia for his tribe. Staying on good terms with Rainbow Serpent, the protector of the lakes and rivers, guarantees that water is plentiful: if respect is not shown to him, drought will follow. These stories are passed down from generation to generation and are remembered, like everything in Aboriginal culture, through storytelling and song. As with other tribal societies animals played a vital role in providing meaning and identity.

The Emu Shaman of central Australia practices his medicine with compresses of herbs and grasses. He also often uses a beautiful green emu egg, passing it over the patient. After doing so, he breaks the egg into a dish and examines it to divine the patient's needs. His body is decorated with white dots of paint and plumage, and he carries an emu-feather fan. The power songs that he performs are accompanied by drumming-like sounds and a glottal booming cry similar to that of the emu.

The Scrub Python Shaman has a weaving, elastic body painted with greenish-brown dots that can be fearsome and startling, and he is said to have gone into other worlds, learned from the snake spirit and returned a shaman. Specialists in renewal, these shamans frequently use snake effigies in their healing work and will "hiss" or blow "snake-breath energy" into a patient. Those being treated have noted a quality of energy surrounding them as being not unlike a strong electrical field. These shamans use healing methods that involve presses, squeezes and kneading, and they often recommend fasting and water treatments. They are noted for their cures for stomach troubles.

The Kangaroo Shaman, or Boomer Shaman, as he is often called, frequently looks back over his shoulder, perhaps to see if an accompanying spirit is there. Mimicking the movements of the kangaroo, his demeanor is an alert wariness. He carries his tools of healing in his kangaroo-fur-lined pouch across his lower stomach, and uses energy enhancements in the form of herbs, bodywork and physical touch to heal his patients.

The Koala Bear Shamans of southeastern Australia are few in number, perhaps because the koala bear itself is endangered. Painted gray with a reddish tinge, they have a stomach pouch stuffed with eucalyptus leaves. They also use eucalyptus fronds as a sort of fan and emit clipped barks in a kind of healing serenade. They work at night in sparse light or in moonlight, carrying out their curative business in shadowy eucalyptus forests.

THE FEATHERED SERPENT AND JAGUAR WAY

Belief in the return of a feathered serpent deity, a god associated with the rising and setting of the planet Venus, is still prevalent among native peoples in southern Mexico, Guatemala and Belize. Quetzalcoatl, one name for the feathered serpent, was the inventor of books, the calendar and maize. Furthermore, several Mesoamerican cultures posited the existence of lines beneath the surface of the earth carrying a flowing snake-like energy that connected all temple mounds, pyramids and other sacred complexes in North and South America. This serpent flow of supernatural power traveled instantly from one sacred site to another. A synergistic connection between earth and sky activated the selected pyramid or mound, and the flying serpent shaman was lifted from the top of the site to the heavens. Afterward, the shaman priests returned to earth, becoming the illuminated emissaries who instructed the people concerning the will of the gods.

Jaguar shape-shifts through many portals, at once king, ruler, shaman, priest and guardian knight. Wearing a fur coat emblazoned with sunspots, he crosses easily into other dimensions and is at home in both the lower and upper worlds. This animal has an important timekeeping significance in the calendar of the Maya, and plays a role in shamanic rituals of fertility and protection. Jaguars range from Mexico to the forests of South America and make rare appearances in New Mexico and Texas in the USA.

In the days before the arrival of the Spanish, an indigenous Mesoamerican shamanism was practiced, often centered around cycles of spiritual regeneration. Priests and divine rulers performed sacrifices, had visions, invented calendar systems, kept records and told magical stories about heroes, detailing how the world came into being. They were monument-builders and architects of great city complexes, and held violent ball games

in large amphitheaters with religious and cosmological significance. The Maya, Aztecs, Toltecs, Olmecs, Mixtecs, Zapotecs and, further south, the Incas and other Mesoamerican cultures have enriched our cultural history, their visionary priests and rulers having been shamans of the first order.

Today, there are master shamans all through Central and South America, encompassing a wide spectrum of established healing techniques and traditions. In Peru, wizards and shamans living on the coast use slices of San Pedro cactus or various hallucinogenic brews in their healing ceremonies. Peruvian shamans also use a snuff made from the seeds of an Andean cloud-forest tree. This psychotropic powder is blown through snuff tubes up the nostrils of the patient, and delivers a surreal jolt. The ego quickly separates and the human self is left behind while the spirit self is catapulted into a place where all riddles are solved – a place of great love and healing.

Psilocybin mushrooms are used in tribal ritual throughout Mexico and South America. Shamans in the rainforest use the potent psychoactive vine ayahuasca to contact the anaconda mother and the jaguar spirits. Out-of-body experiences are not uncommon and visitations of ancestor spirits often occur when this brew is ingested. Deer and hummingbird spirits hover around peyote ceremonies, so it is told by elders and shamans. All these shamanic techniques have the power to transform and to heal.

THE FOOD OF THE GODS

One mythic story tells of the feathered serpent god Quetzalcoatl descending to earth on a ray of light from the planet Venus. He brought with him a stolen cocoa tree from the starry Elysian Fields, and from the seed of this tree an unsweetened spiced beverage was made. Because of chocolate's mythical origins, it was known as the food of the gods, and cocoa pods were considered holy, figuring in much shamanic ritual. Cocoa was believed to confer wisdom and health, and the aphrodisiacal qualities of the drink were not missed either. Cocoa beans were also used as currency and regarded as a form of wealth.

CONTEMPORARY SHAMANISM

Traditional shamanism is usually highly secretive. It is practiced in tribal societies that follow long-cherished beliefs about the nature of reality. Secrecy shuts the door on access to this body of specialized information. Tribal people have become justifiably sceptical about sharing their knowledge with outsiders, their beliefs often being at odds with modernity. So why has shamanism become so important to our contemporary society? One simple reason is that the practice of shamanism unites people with nature.

We live in a cultural and historical milieu that insulates us from the natural world, and with every technological advance we are shunted further away from our natural evolution. But contemporary shamanism can bring us back into contact with our innermost being and with higher states of consciousness. We can connect with our fellow creatures, the animals – and we have already seen how they can teach us many lessons, including problem-solving, healing, growth and self-understanding, even in today's complex world.

Animals are at the heart of any authentic shamanism. Contemporary shamans today are busy with their animal spirit helpers, mending the ripped-up fabric of our time, trying to guide the wobbling spaceship Earth and maintain the cosmic balance. They are stitching patchwork over holes and mending the tattered edges. They do this by rites and rituals, visioning, praying, dreaming and working inside the spirit world. The more our world unravels, the more we will need our shamans. Perhaps, as a species, we need spiritual connection and guidance from our animistic nature as never before. We need our rites of passage and the ideal of an eco-friendly world. So let the shamans of our time step forward and bring us their nurture and their love.

The Spirit of the Shaman

In the distance . . .
We hear the drumbeat – the dancebeat.
Holding her eagle-wing fan
An old woman bends forward
And dips the tip into water from a sacred spring.
She flicks it in the four directions.
She prays to oceans, lakes, rivers and mountain mists.
She prays to all life and all creatures in it.
She touches her fan to the tree
And standing under the stars that night
She sings a power song and calls her animal helpers to her.

CHAPTER 1

Working with Animal Spirits

This chapter will give you practical guidance on how to find the animal spirit that will be most helpful to you as you progress in your spiritual development. Through meditation, visualization and other forms of spiritual quest, your animal will make itself known to you.

Animals have magical abilities to heal the body, mind and spirit. They are adaptable and clever, level-headed and decisive, and their skills have been honed by experience. They can therefore help you make momentous decisions. Animals are spontaneous, engaging with every situation full of awareness, and their behavior is always direct and straightforward. They can lead you to self-trust, and teach you self-reliance and fearlessness. Now begins the work to connect you with your animal spirits.

THE INNER QUEST

On an inner quest we aim to find out who we really are, to find our true spirit. For some people religious inspiration is the key motivation for their inner journey. Others use quiet meditation to calm or silence the mind to nothingness in order to hear the heart's truth. This practice of going within allows us to hear the voice not of the mind but of the spirit. This is the voice that calls us and tells us the truth of who we are and guides us in every step of our journey.

This spirit voice can also come through the appearance of animal messengers in our lives. Animal power is the power of nature. It is a sublime and mysterious force that has been known and harnessed by indigenous cultures for many centuries. Animals are the conduits of energy and knowledge by which the mysterious unknown communicates with us. Their appearances are the signs that our intent and the sincerity of our inner quest have been honored and recognized by the world of spirit. They are the indicators that we are going beyond our material selves and entering another place altogether.

Animal spirits can work invisibly in alliance with each of us in a way reminiscent of the traditional powers of guardian angels. Each spirit most commonly provides a protective shield against illness and negative energies, including dangerous emotions such as anger and jealousy. The spirit also makes available to the individual its own specialized form of virtue or wisdom. In simplified terms, a lion spirit will give you something of the character of a lion – independence, courage and self-belief (see page 68) – while a hawk spirit will give you far-sighted perceptiveness as well as mental and emotional nimbleness (see page 52). Shamans often say that without one or two of these guardian power animals, no one would be able to survive the hard knocks of childhood. Over the course of a lifetime, a succession of animal spirits may be operating.

THE VISION QUEST

One traditional Native American path for finding spiritual guidance is through the vision quest. This is a kind of rite of passage, often at the onset of puberty. Individuals would first purify themselves by bathing or visiting a sweat lodge. They would then journey to an isolated place and camp there for several days of fasting and prayer – of "crying for a vision". This is a quest for a powerful spirit guide, a supernatural being, a sacred helper, a benefactor. Normally, this is an animal. It may be a raccoon, a hummingbird, a coyote, a snake, an eagle or a bird as humble as a sparrow or a chickadee. Or perhaps a deer or elk will come. The animal will speak to the seeker and instruct him or her; it can highlight a sacred path and show how to gain power and find excellence in this world.

Often a vision quest takes place within a circle or a ring in a hidden place – a sacred space. The seeker enters the circle from the east and may acknowledge the energy of each of the four directions in turn. The east is honored for the eastern light, the power of the rising sun; the south is honoured for warmth and comfort and the spirit of youthfulness; the west is acknowledged as the place of dreams, visions and dark matter; the north is the place of the snow and the mountain, inner wisdom and rediscovering immortal truths.

For untold centuries the vision quest has taken place – the sacrifice, the quest, the way of knowing and understanding, and of finding personal power through animal spirit guidance. It is a timeworn rite arriving as the new generations come, flowing in and out of time. The tradition of the vision quest is carefully preserved. There will always be a spiritual interface with animals as long as there are vision quests.

FINDING YOUR ANIMAL TOTEM

There are a number of ways to discover your animal totem, and we'll explore these in the next few pages. Meditations, dreams or your own version of a traditional vision quest can all be very effective methods.

You may believe that you have consciously chosen a power animal, but often a deep intuitive empathy will be invisibly at work, guiding your choice. Some people look at photographs or artworks of different animals, rendered in a consistent style, and opt for the creature to which they show the strongest response. However, it is usually better to select your power animal by being open to signals, from whatever source, than by a deliberate act of recruitment, which may be contaminated by a conscious liking for glamorous or fashionable animals.

Domesticated animals, such as cows or sheep, are not usually thought of as power animals because they are subordinate to human beings. However, an exception may be made for cats, dogs and aviary birds, as these are not too far removed, genetically and in terms of temperament, from their wild ancestors. Indeed, it can be helpful to experiment with a cat or a dog (see pages 54 and 84) as a totem before progressing to a more involved level with, say, a jaguar or a wolf (see pages 60 and 66). Real cats and dogs can play a part in this process: they have their own strong energies, from which you can gain helpful practice. An animal totem is a part of your personal heritage. If you work with your totem animal you will soon learn to trust its guidance.

GIVING THANKS

Once you have found your spirit animal it is very important to offer gratitude to develop and maintain the relationship. In shamanism, the hunter always honors the prey in a ritual ceremony both before and after the taking of life. It is also important to honor the animal that freely provides the benefit of its time and energy. In the process of giving thanks, we gain a closer connection. One way to express our appreciation is through a simple affirmation, which may be spoken aloud or voiced inwardly. Another way is to display a small sculpture or model of the creature – a kind of miniature altar. Some people find that three-dimensional representations tend to generate stronger energies than two-dimensional ones, but you may well wish to challenge this assumption if, for example, you are displaying a beautiful Japanese print of a flying crane or heron.

Prehistoric shamans used sympathetic magic in their cave paintings of animals to summon spirits to aid them, knowing full well that the flesh and blood animals would soon follow. An element of reverence and thanksgiving was inherent in these representations. To offer thanks to your animal totem, consider any or all of the following gestures:

Recite a text in gratitude Recite (or voice inwardly) a text that perfectly captures the qualities of the animal whenever you are feeling especially grateful – and certainly whenever you feel you have benefited from your animal totem's help.

Express a direct thank you Alternatively, you can use a text to summon your totem to give them personal thanks. An example might be English poet and artist William Blake's powerful poem beginning, "Tiger, tiger, burning bright/In the forests of the night."

Display an image Some traditional cultures prolifically produce carvings of animals important to them – for example, deer carvings may be easy to find in woodland areas or graceful depictions of birds in Chinese and Japanese prints. Drawing your own representation is a way to give thanks for a particular act of assistance. It may also deepen your connection with the animal's energies.

WORKING WITH DREAMS

Dreams can be among the most effective ways of finding and connecting with your power animal. When we dream, our conscious mind – the part that can prevent us from accessing our hidden thoughts and feelings – closes down. The subconscious is the realm of deepest emotions – our most powerful wishes but also our most profound fears and anxieties. This is a good place from which to summon a power animal, a spirit being that expresses your innermost needs.

According to the psychologist Carl Jung, in addition to the personal unconscious, humans also possess another level of the unconscious mind, the collective unconscious. This, he believed, was where shared ideas and beliefs across all humanity are found – archetypes or symbols of such important concepts as mother and father, wise ruler and hero. This is where you may find the spirit animal that most powerfully communicates to you – an animal that speaks across different cultures and societies.

Many dream experts claim that there are three levels of dreams, which correspond to these different levels of the unconscious. Level One dreams draw from recognizable events from the previous day or in recent memory and may help you to deal with unfinished business or resolve troubling questions. Level Two dreams draw from deeper within our personal unconscious, and can help us explore aspects of our essential character and nature. Level Three dreams tend to be far rarer. Jung believed that they carry tremendous wisdom and mystical guidance, helping us to connect with the divine. This may be your power animal dream.

Whichever level of dream you experience, a vision of any animal in a dream is extremely important and may reveal the qualities or inner characteristics that you need to develop or explore further.

Incubating a Power Animal Dream

Researchers have found that it is possible to encourage a dream on a particular topic by concentrating on the issue on a regular basis before going to sleep. To encourage your own power animal to visit you in a dream, take time each night to focus on the animal world.

1 Sit in a comfortable position and close your eyes. Breathe deeply and slowly, taking time to fully relax.

2 Allow your mind to range freely over the concept of spirit animals. Give full reign to the associations the concept brings up, following threads however odd or incongruous they may seem. Simply spend time with the animal world in your head.

3 Continue to breathe deeply. Repeat to yourself three times, "Tonight I ask that my power animal may visit me."

4 To close the ceremony, thank the world of spirit for any vision you may receive, whatever form it takes.

WORKING WITH A CREATIVE VISUALIZATION

Creative visualization is another very effective way to discover your power animal. Creative visualization can also be described as guided meditation. It involves taking your mind on a journey and, during the process, circumventing the conscious or controlling part of the mind and accessing deeper, unconscious concerns. The aim of the visualization on the opposite page is to help you connect deeply with the natural world, gaining a heightened awareness in particular of animals that may represent something important within your subconscious.

Find a quiet place where you won't be disturbed and begin by closing your eyes and taking a few deep, slow breaths until you feel calm and relaxed. You may find it helpful to record the visualization in advance and play it back to yourself.

A Power Animal Visualization

1 In your mind's eye take yourself into a lovely spring meadow, dotted with wildflowers. You can hear birds singing, a gentle breeze is blowing and it is pleasantly warm. Stand still for a moment enjoying the peace and serenity that surrounds you. You can not only hear the birds, you can see them now too, darting above the grasses and winging through the air. Take note of the birds you can see. What do they look like? What color are they?

2 At the edge of the meadow is a wood. You follow a path through the meadow, aware of the hum of insects. Looking down you see a whole world unfold before you – dragonflies, crickets, beetles and ants. Take time to study all you can see before you enter the wood.

3 It is cool and quiet beneath the trees and your eyes have to adjust to the dimmer light. You tread carefully, not wanting to disturb any creatures that might be taking refuge. All at once you reach a clearing, illuminated by a shaft of light. At the center of the clearing stands a woodland animal which gazes back at you as you quietly approach. What kind of animal is it? Describe it to yourself in detail. Is it large or small? What color is it? Be sure to thank the animal for appearing before you.

4 You walk still deeper into the wood. Beside you is a bubbling stream. You hear a plop – something has disappeared beneath the surface of the water. Is it a fish, or perhaps a frog? Focus on the clear water. Maybe you have seen an otter, a beaver or even a platypus?

5 It is time to go home now. Follow the path back through the ferns, past the clearing and out into the meadow. You are back among the singing birds, the hum of insects, the grasses and flowers gently blowing in the breeze. You are back where you started. Open your eyes.

6 Give thanks for all you have seen on this journey, and breathe deeply and slowly as you start to relax again.

7 Write down in a journal your experiences. In particular, pay attention to any animal that was especially clear to you during your visualization or that made a major impact. Perhaps this is your power animal.

USING RITUAL AND CEREMONY TO DISCOVER YOUR POWER ANIMAL

The vision quest (see page 25) is a powerful tool for revealing your spirit guide. Even if you live in a large city, it is possible to adapt its principles to create your own vision experience.

A Modern-day Vision Quest

Ideally you would travel to an isolated location for your vision quest but this may not be possible, so this one is based around your own home. Choose a weekend when you have no commitments and will be able to spend a significant amount of time alone.

1 Begin preparing for your quest on a Friday evening. Give some thought to what you will eat over the weekend. Traditionally, vision seekers would fast in order to purify themselves. An actual fast where you eat nothing for a lengthy period can be dangerous and should not be undertaken without medical advice. However, you could restrict the kinds of food you eat – for example, you might eat only fruits and vegetables and drink plenty of water, avoiding tea, coffee and alcohol.

2 Native Americans cleansed themselves before a vision quest by bathing or spending time in a sweat lodge. In the same way you may like to take a ritual shower or bath. Use a pumice stone or exfoliator to slough off dry skin. This has important ritual meaning – literally you are shedding old ways of being to allow new experiences to take place.

3 You could also explore the tradition of smudging. This involves bathing in the smoke of cleansing and healing herbs. Use an abalone shell, an iron skillet or even a tin can as a holder in which to burn power plants. Burn sage to banish bad spirits and bring good energy; sweetgrass for the sweetness of life; osha root for endurance; cedar for a long life; red willow bark to enhance prayers; mullein for courage; buck brush to move stagnant energy; and copal to please ancestor spirits.

4 Now is the time to give thought to where your vision quest will take place. You need to find a place where you can sit peacefully and quietly, undisturbed for at least an hour at a time. Ideally you would choose an outside place in order to better connect with the natural world. Is there a dark, quiet corner in your garden where you could mark out a circle with stones, for example? If you don't have access to outside space, you could create a vision circle in a quiet room in your home. Collect some items to connect your circle to the natural world – for example, some leaves fallen from a tree, some feathers or wildflowers you've gathered. Mark out a circle with some crystals or other natural objects.

5 Establish where the four directions fall on your circle and mark each point with an object that represents the energy of that direction. For example, you could choose a different colored candle for each of the directions. The colors of the candles are important: red for health and passion; yellow for perfecting the intellect; black for banishing bad energy; white for spiritual purity; green for prosperity; blue for healing; and purple to increase spiritual power.

6 Enter your circle from the east and acknowledge each of the directions in turn. Now sit quietly within your sacred circle and close your eyes. Breathe deeply and ask that your power animal make itself known to you. Ideally you should remain within your circle for as long as possible: the minimum time is an hour. It may be difficult at first to remain still for this long, but you need to allow space for your spirit to rise and express itself.

Your vision could come at any point during the weekend, but it is important to keep returning to the sacred circle over the course of the two days. As you go further into silence and isolation, more will be revealed.

At the end of your weekend, write down in your journal all you have experienced and learned.

MEDITATION

If you have now found your spirit animal, you can begin to explore ways of working with your helper. Remember your guide may well take the initiative, leading you to insights or experiences beyond your conscious control. One very powerful way in which you can draw closer to your spirit guide is through meditation.

By meditating on the various talents and attributes of your power animal you can begin to connect with and share these energies. Put yourself in alignment with your power animal's energy, shamanize within your meditation and ask your animal to instruct you. For example, if you are seeking prosperity, meditate on the qualities of the buffalo (see page 78). If you want to reach out to the web of life, meditate on spider (see page 64). If you want strength, ask for the power of horse to come to you in your meditation (see page 86).

Meditation provides real benefit for weathering the stresses of our times. Tensions fall away and are replaced with peacefulness. Though internal, meditation helps you deal with the problems of everyday life. It centers and calms you, and puts you in touch with intuitive knowledge. Meditation also facilitates coming to terms with change. It sweeps the mind clear of all unnecessary baggage and provides clarity. At its most profound level it can reveal the divinity within – your animal spirit can help you as you travel this path.

Starting to Meditate

If you are new to meditation there are a few simple rules to follow to help you get the most from this practice.

1. It is important to find a quiet and peaceful place where you can sit undisturbed for at least 20 minutes. You may find it helpful to minimize all distractions by drawing the curtains, closing the doors and windows and ensuring all phones and computers are switched off.
2. The aim is to be relaxed yet alert, so sit in a comfortable position with your back as straight as possible so that you can breathe deeply and easily. The traditional pose is to sit cross-legged, although not everyone finds this easy to do. Another option is to sit kneeling on a cushion. Alternatively, find a straight-backed chair and sit with your hands resting on your knees. Lying down is not recommended as there is the danger you may fall asleep!
3. The aim of meditation is to clear the mind of all the busy thoughts and concerns that can prevent us from seeing things more clearly. When the mind is still and calm you can gain profound insights. One common approach to help still the mind is to focus on your breathing, counting slowly up from one to four as you inhale and down from four to one as you exhale. Your mind may well want to wander away and on to other concerns; whenever this happens, gently steer it back to counting as you inhale and exhale. Continue doing this for 5 to 10 minutes.
4. You can now gently bring into focus your spirit animal. Allow it to take whatever form it chooses in your mind. You may see it as a sleeping form, its energies dormant, charged with latent power. Try not to question the image but simply observe it. When you mind is relaxed and calm, your animal may bring you special messages and insights. The message may be subtle, or not apparent at all at first. Try to remain open and receptive; don't question what comes to you, simply accept it. A deeper meaning may emerge in time.
5. When you are ready to end your meditation session, give yourself time to return to normality. Count yourself slowly back to full alertness and allow a period of adjustment afterward.

HEALING WITH ANIMAL SPIRITS

Healing with animal spirits was the norm in Native America until Western medical practice began to undermine the model in the 16th century. Shamans taught that animals brought and defined disease. Symptoms were seen to mimic animals – so the way an arthritis sufferer may be bent forward and aided by two walking sticks was seen as similar to the way a deer walks. The patient did not suffer from crippling arthritis but deer disease.

In legend, the deer spirit first brought sickness to humans when a hunter killed the animal. Deer said, "You have not acknowledged me or my spirit. For this insult, I am giving you a disease, but I will also give you the cure. I am letting you [the shaman] have a little part of my breath to blow upon the body of the sick person. This and other secret methods I will tell you will be the treatment for this affliction [arthritis]."

There were hundreds of animal-linked diseases, such as fox sickness, millipede sickness, grouse sickness (also called little-gray-smoke sickness), eagle sickness and rabbit sickness.

Illness was caused by imbalance between people and the animals, and the offended animals taught the way to heal the sickness that they had caused. The power doctor standing in a doctoring circle called animal and helping spirits into the circle. She used her doctor eyes – a sort of shaman's X-ray – to look into the patient. Perhaps she saw a sick animal at the site of the illness – for example, in the stomach or inside the chest – such as an ailing snake, signifying cobralita sickness. Little-snake sickness is the onset of curvature of the spine. In consultation with the snake, the power doctor learned the exact cause. With treatment, the sickness would dissipate and the body would be repaired and good health restored.

SELF-HEALING SONG AND DANCE

Animals, our first teachers, assist in self-healing. Ask your spirit animal to give you a song to aid you – an energizing song of personal empowerment. Perhaps you could begin by chanting some repetitive utterances associated with indigenous music. Let the repetitive quality of your voice touch your deepest spiritual knowing. Let the chant veer off in any direction it wants until it links with a response of inner uplift, a strength-bringing wisdom that is grounded and real.

Find your power animal song, a power song you can sing on the road to self-healing. Few song lyrics mention bears, gazelles, dolphins or hares, so it is best to judge the song by the rhythms or by the sound of the words rather than by their meaning. Sibilant sounds might be suitable for a cat, growling sounds – or a howling blues – for a wolf. Alternatively, find some music that puts you into a mood of spiritual unity and listen to it. If you feel you are in a locked cycle of dis-ease, a new melody can break you free.

Add to this an animal power dance. Let the spirit of your animal live and breathe through you. Acknowledge and dance with your spirit animal; become aware and listen. Dance is a method of hearing what your body is telling you, and synchronizing it with higher truth.

MASK OF THE EARTH: ALTARS AND SACRED SPACE

Mask of the earth is a shamanic term for an altar, a place of prayer and reverence. There are many kinds of altar. Here we are speaking of a personal or home altar, which can be very helpful when working with spirit animals. It provides a focus for your spiritual work and can concentrate your energies.

Set up an altar in a consecrated place in your home. Sweep the area clean of bad energy by smudging (see page 32), and mark it as a barrier against negative outside energies. Energize the space with heightened awareness, prayer, contemplation, meditation and chanting.

Place in the east pictures of spiritual teachers, ascended masters, bowls of (holy) water, religious icons or any item that may draw spiritual power to you. Seven white candles at the very back of your altar will act as antennae, balancing the energy of your array of power objects.

The south should hold your personal power objects, such as photographs and awards – ordinary things that bring you into consensus with reality and establish trust. You could include items from your childhood if you like.

The west is the place for ancestral objects, relics and sacrificial incense – anything that connects you with the dreamtime or your inner world. Include items that connect you with your ambitions or other wishes.

In the north put pictures of elders, and earth and space items such as loadstones, meteorites, rocks, gemstones or any small object that an elder has given you. Here place items that energize you as well as those that remind you of old age and your spiritual obligation to obtain sacred knowledge and become wise.

Altars acknowledge all forces. They are designed to connect with the nervous system of the universe and are collectors of universal intelligence. The powers of the universe come together on the altar at a point in the here and the now. Long ago there was a break, a schism between the animals and humans – a tragic alienation. An altar creates a bridge, inviting these vanished beings back into your world.

A Spiritual Habitat

Another approach is to furnish the area around your altar in a way that you deem appropriate to the animal you wish to summon. If your intent is to acquire spiritual vision, you might seek an eagle for help, for example, and in this situation you might place your altar in the highest room of the home. Use a little ingenuity to create a suitably embellished sacred space in which to work with your spirit animal – a spiritual habitat for you and your wild companion. Use natural features such as branches, shells, feathers and flowers as the starting-point, then see where your imagination takes you.

OVERCOMING OBSTACLES

Consult your power animal when you are faced with seemingly insurmountable obstacles or insoluble problems. Animals have a long history of helping humans to vanquish difficulties or answer urgent needs: cats to catch rats, dogs to protect and warn, horses to carry goods and to move you from place to place, pigeons to send long-distance messages, and so on. Even problems that appear to be so nebulous or entrenched that you don't know how to begin to tackle them can often be translated into terms that suggest the appropriate animal helper. For example, if you find that resentment has infiltrated your relationship, you might enlist a dove to carry an olive branch of peace to your loved one.

Obstacles are obstructions similar to walls. An eagle or a hawk could fly over a wall. A prairie dog could burrow under it. Unless it is the Great Wall of China, many animals could efficiently make their way around it. A team of horses could probably demolish it. Tell your power animal all about your obstacle and see what advice is forthcoming. Perhaps you can solve your problem straight away. If not, try the following approaches:

- **Define your obstacle** Ask yourself, "What exactly is it?"
- **Take responsibility** In the world of cause and effect, you are both.
- **Make a start** Begin by clearing small obstacles.
- **Do not ruminate – act** Do what you can and then stop worrying.
- **Become one with the solution** Ask the Highest Power to move you into the answer zone. You will know when all is as it should be.
- **Learn from animals** Obstacles are spiritual lessons – approach them with that understanding. If you are trying to break the power of an obstacle with your obstinacy, stop. Relax, take some deep breaths and let go of the struggle. What is the easiest path to understanding your lesson and moving on? Remember that animals are decisive: they act instinctively and quickly.

A Wheel of Animal Guidance

Native Americans often utilize the sacred wheel for answering questions and solving dilemmas. We can also move around the wheel and visit the animals in the three cardinal directions of east, west and south; in the north we make a prayer and then we go to the sacred tree in the center of the wheel for resolution. Consult with the animals of each direction about your problem, obstacle, situation, quest or dilemma. Remember to thank each animal for their counsel.

1. Sit somewhere comfortable where you will not be disturbed. In the east, ask Coyote Jester your question. You are going to get a flippant answer. Beware of hidden meanings, *double entendres* or cryptic communications from this animal. Thank the coyote for its help.
2. Go to the south on the wheel and ask Chasing Wolf, a great warrior animal, about tactics to use against any opposition you may encounter. Ask this great warrior how to stalk the answer to your question or problem. Thank the wolf.
3. In the west, ask Toad Woman your question. She may reveal to you the sinister truth that lies beneath your dilemma. Shadowy old Toad Woman may tell you your hidden agenda for asking the question in the first place. Thank Toad Woman.
4. Now go to the north and pray for resolution. Go to the sacred tree in the center of the wheel, remember the advice of each animal and pray once more. It is here that you must take your personal authority and make your decision.

WALKING WITH YOUR ANIMAL SPIRIT

Do you remember the animals of your childhood, how they inspired and awed you? Animals from the movies, cartoons, television and books mirrored the conduct of human beings. Tales from Aesop, the Brothers Grimm and Walt Disney brought enchantment and humor. Animal stories acquainted us with our own potential and characteristics. Mouse (Mickey), deer (Bambi), horse (Flicka), cat (Sylvester), crows (Heckel and Jeckel), dog (Lassie), pig (Porky), duck (Donald), tiger (Tony), moose (Bullwinkle), elephant (Dumbo), woodpecker (Woody), rabbit (Bugs Bunny) – all these animals were used to demonstrate behavior, both good and bad.

From around the world came stories of animals. From tribal and folk cultures to the most industrialized societies, stories of fabled animals taught us about our strengths and weaknesses in a predatory world, gave us moral courage, inspired us and hinted that all of us have astonishing powers at our command. Today, we still have much to learn from animals. Reconnect and bring the presence of your spirit animal into your ordinary, everyday affairs. Be aware, turn back the clock, remember and rebalance with the circle of all of life.

Walk with your spirit animal. Ask your spirit animal to be with you as you go about your business. Ask your spirit animal to give you nudges in the right direction. Remember, we are all on a journey to the spirit world. Ask your spirit animal to give you the treasures of spirit.

IMAGINATION AND AFFIRMATIONS

Working together, your imagination and your ability to powerfully affirm your intent can help you to access animal energy.

Imagination You can imagine whatever you like, whenever you like. But there is a downside – you can imagine the bad as well as the good. The imagination is not unlike a movie projected on the screen of your mind. You have the possibility to project the positive or the negative, according to your mood or temperament, sickness or health, poverty or prosperity, and so on. The movies to which you give top billing are likely to leak their energies into your life for good or bad.

Animals bring force and power to your imagining and dreaming. Be highly observant of the animals that come to you in dreams. These are truly power symbols (see page 28). For example, if a grizzly bear visits your dreamtime, perhaps it is a sign that you are sleeping on an issue (see page 70). A fierce bear may signal for you to become more aggressive and master your fears. Such a dream would be an important, powerful message, and it would be a good idea to find a bear fetish or talisman to remind you that this animal's energy is with you.

Affirmations Affirmations are positive nods to the universe that you are serious about your quest for greater spiritual meaning in life. Affirmations are the stamps on the letters of intent – they send the message to its mark. Intent originates in the brain; affirmations, especially if spoken aloud, cement the intent into reality. The human voice contains tremendous power to manifest into form. Affirmations can harness this power and can actualize your intent. Intend your power animal to come to you while saying aloud phrases such as, "I honour all animals. I welcome and invite my power animal to come to me now and make itself known to me." This type of daily ceremony will not only result in an animal spirit visiting you, but will affirm your own mission. As you hear the positive power of your own voice, you will be supported in your quest to connect and work with your power animal.

CHAPTER 2

Inner Qualities

The fast pace of the world we live in – the demands of the workplace, technological change and financial pressures – makes it easy to forget our kinship with animals. It is even easier to neglect our own inner animal spirit, from which we can find strength, wisdom and guidance.

There are various ways to reconnect with our inner guides. One is to make a conscious effort to find the creature that counterbalances the weaknesses we perceive within ourselves – for example, a lion might help us with timidity. Another approach is to identify one or more animals with which we feel a special affinity and work closely with those creatures on a whole range of issues and anxieties. This chapter explores the animals that can offer special insights into our character and psyche.

SNAKE

THE IMMORTAL HEALER

Snake is considered a creature possessed of supernatural powers in many shamanic societies. It carries the energy of water, and shamans often meditate with the snake spirit to learn ways to combat drought. A good relationship with snakes is essential to keep corn and other plants growing in an arid environment. Shamans use their power to communicate with snakes, seeking advice concerning the rituals that must be carried out to please the snake spirits and make sure crops remain healthy and growing. Although Australian Aborigines did not cultivate crops, in that culture, too, the snake was considered important. The concept of the Rainbow Serpent, a powerful creature, both creative and dangerous, is found in the traditions of a wide range of tribes (see page 16). Rainbow Serpent was often found in waterholes and rivers and was associated with rainmaking and healing powers.

Snakes can cast off their skin: in effect, the old skin is turned inside out as the snake wiggles out of it. Older snakes shed their skin once or twice a year, but younger snakes can do this up to four times a year. This ability to shed the skin has fascinated cultures around the world: the snake has come to be seen as a symbol of renewal, rebirth and healing. The ouroboros symbol, a snake eating its own tail, is found in many cultures, and represents this concept of regeneration and immortality.

Snake carries a powerful energy. This energy can be the key to past lives, portals of wisdom or even a soul guide leading an individual to freedom. Snake is a master of quick strikes and of internal energy. The creature is agile and supple and has great cunning. In the Judeo-Christian tradition, snake is a trickster, bringing sin into the world, but in other traditions it is associated with the earth goddess, fertility and sexual energy.

Awakening the Serpent

In yogic tradition, the snake is seen as embodying Shakti, the divine female cosmic energy. This force is known as kundalini, and is envisaged as a coiled serpent lying dormant at the base of the spine. When kundalini energy is awakened by energizing in turn each of the major chakras, or subtle energy centers, that lie along the spine, it is believed we can attain divine wisdom and experience cosmic one-ness.

This meditation focuses on each chakra in turn and can help you tune into kundalini.

1 Find a quiet place, sit in a comfortable position, close your eyes and relax.

2 Begin by focusing on your base chakra, located at the base of the spine. It keeps us grounded and connected.

3 Next is your sacral chakra, located below the navel. Focus on its creative energy.

4 Feel the energy rise to the third chakra, the solar plexus, between the navel and the sternum. Feel the energy of growth and expansiveness.

5 Progress to the heart chakra, found near the sternum. Feel the energy of passion and devotion.

6 Move up to the fifth chakra, the throat, found between the collar bone and the larynx. Experience the power of communication.

7 Feel the energy rise to the brow chakra, the sixth, found in the center of the forehead. Sense your capacity for intuition and clarity.

8 Now progress to the last chakra, the crown chakra, at the top of the head. This is the place of universal consciousness and cosmic one-ness. Open yourself to these powers.

9 Close the meditation by revisiting each chakra in turn, feeling the energy balanced and harmonious.

MOLE

GOING BENEATH

Moles, hedgehogs and shrews belong to the Talpidae family. Do not think of mole as a traitor, sell-out, spy or double agent. Instead, think of the subterranean mole as earthy – it gets down under the ground and explores beneath the surface of things. Moles know about seeds breaking open and seeking light – the genesis of plant life. They know more about the roots than they do about branches.

Moles are the keepers of the many kinds of soil. They know the sacred soils as well as the toxic ones. They know that certain soils are good for some people and bad for others. They know about fertile soils and about the dead earth that will grow nothing. Because they live mostly underground, moles are close to the ancestors. Ask mole to lead you through its secret tunnels to the soil that sustains you and awakens your spirit. You seek a place of nourishment, growth and new beginnings – a place to rekindle your heart and soul.

To dig into the earth, you must get yourself dirty, and mole magic opens up new possibilities. You may have to dig for answers, but mole has got them for you, though they may not be the *obvious* answers. Mole can help you find those things you have hidden from yourself – things that you have repressed and may not even want to know.

Moles symbolize the deepest recesses of the subconscious mind. They know the passages and chambers in the dark interior of the earth, and are guides through the secret labyrinths of the mind. Moles teach you to go beneath and seek knowledge from a deeper place.

Because moles burrow into the fertile earth, they are often associated with fertility. Their eyes are small, sunken and hidden in fur. They are nearly blind yet they are masters of the darkness, and because of this they are used in witchcraft and sorcery. Many a witch's brew contains a mole hair.

SACRED MOLE DIRT

Mole dirt is the earth that is thrown up in mounds around mole tunnel entrances. A bed of this dirt is often used to make traditional altars in Native American cultures. Mole dirt connects to all the energies of inner earth. Using this dirt in altar building symbolizes and makes a connection with the life-bringing powers of the Earth Mother and the regeneration of life. On this altar place symbolic representations of the supernatural forces being contacted. For example, an owl fetish might be placed on a moon altar. The moon's chief helper on earth is the owl, so the moon may well send messages in dreams via this mysterious bird.

There are many tales concerning sacred mole dirt. In one Native American tale, a man called Gray Hawk was walking in the early hours of the morning on the prairie when he heard a noise – "scritch-scritch". He looked down and saw that dirt was being tossed up into a mound. A mole appeared and there was a strange form of miniature lightning – electric snakes of blue light – around the earth he had thrown up. The mole rose and adopted the form of a blind man. He took Gray Hawk by the arm and said, "I have waited for you and today I will adopt you as my son. You will have my power."

The blind man was suddenly holding a hoop in front of him. "Look through it," he said. When Gray Hawk looked, he saw a distant village of an enemy tribe. "By this hoop, you will always know where your enemies are and when they are coming. They will not be able to fool you. Make a hoop like this of red willow covered in wolf skin. Keep it wrapped in a pretty blanket. Whenever you want to see the enemy, get fresh mole dirt, put it on the ground, make a smudge and unwrap your blanket. Hold the hoop with both hands and pass it through the smoke. Place it on the mole dirt and then pick it up. Do this four times, pressing the medicine hoop to your breast. When you look into the hoop, you will know everything."

This vision hoop was always accurate when telling of the enemy and became a famous method of divination among the people. The warriors always had great foresight and struck the enemy with a vengeance.

TURTLE
IN TUNE WITH THE COSMOS

In Native American mythology, turtle supported the first human – a woman who fell from the sky. At that time there was only water and no earth. Turtle came up from the depths, and birds caught the falling woman and set her gently on turtle's back. The water stirred up and became land, and so Turtle Island was born. The tribes that settled on Turtle Island were called the Turtle Nations.

Turtle is the primeval one – enduring, experienced and knowing. In fact, turtle is so old that her body is still in harmony with the will of the cosmos. Turtle is the chief of all the animals with shells. Turtle shells have been employed in reading the future: they carry the stamp of the cosmos and were used in many systems of divination, most notably the ancient Chinese book of divination, the *I Ching*. In this system the markings on the shell were seen as yin and yang symbols – of negative and positive, feminine and masculine. Seers began to see and understand the hidden and accurate meanings within the interplay of yin and yang imprinted upon turtle's back.

Turtle tells you to trust your intuition. Look for inspiration from the turtle as well as the ability to proceed slowly while getting the job done steadily. Turtle's front legs are powerful and they can plow through almost any difficult situation.

When you correctly understand turtle's capabilities, you can overcome indecision. Turtle always has the answer. Turtle teaches us to protect our personal space and how to shield ourselves from negative energies. You may also learn longevity secrets associated with the turtle that relate to this animal's ancient connection with the earth and the cosmos. Turtle's yoking of the upper world with the lower world will help you to discover the gift of a long and prosperous life.

A Great Black Turtle Exercise

Turtle is the architect of the world. According to ancient seers, the domed shell of the turtle, the top carapace, is a map that encompasses the entire universe. The lighter-colored bottom, the "plastron" of the shell, connects with earth. When you do this exercise, try not to think. Try to discover, to be, to become. The ideal is to become one with the cosmos, even for an instant.

1 First, lie comfortably on your stomach on the floor, with your head in the direction of north. See if you can feel the dragon streak, the lightning in the earth. If so, let it flow from south to north. If not, don't think about it. Just let yourself become balanced, comfortable and relaxed.

2 There are many bodies hidden within the physical body, and the turtle is one of them. Let go and allow your mind to wander in dream images – dream that you are a cosmic turtle. Imagine now that you have a turtle's indestructible body – a creature of strength, endurance and longevity. You are the old one, the slow and knowing one – the immortal one.

3 Imagine the black dome of the night sky filled with stars – the sweet black waters of space. Expand your turtle body so that the dome of the sky is your protective shell. Let your "turtleness" become the universe. Confirm yourself as the center and become the universal merging point from where your center originates. When you find your center, you'll find that you are the cosmos within the cosmos you are seeking. You have become one with the great black turtle and have experienced your own immortality.

HAWK

PENETRATING VISION

If you want to imply that someone is sharp, on their toes and acutely aware, you might say that they have eyes like a hawk. Are you viewing your life with keen and penetrating eyes? Are you assessing your situation accurately? Do you need to be more observant? Do you see your goals clearly? Hawk is a fine detective, seeing everything, every clue and nuance, and accurately assessing the situation. If you feel bewildered, use the hawk's totem power for penetrating vision. Learn to see with the eyes of a hawk.

The clear-eyed hawk is observant and sees deeply into the patterns and designs of our world, no matter how well camouflaged. The hawk knows what events are hatching. Hawk, like eagle, is a solar bird that can gaze unflinching into the sun. He sees the hovering spirits nearby and confers with them, and these communications often tell of future events. The hawk is a great prophet bird and a grand oracle. Listen to what your hawk totem tells you.

In Egypt, the hawk was sacred to the solar gods and goddesses, and the penalty for killing a hawk was death. A hawk was released and flew into the sky at the funeral rites of pharaohs. The sight of the hawk signified that his soul had left his body and he had passed into the spirit world.

Hawk is a keen-sighted visionary, a tracer, a detective and solver of riddles. If you had the visual acuity of a hawk, you could read this book from over a mile away. When a hawk is circling high over his prey, the lenses of his eyes are like telescopes, but by the time they are in close proximity, they are like microscopes.

THE EYE OF HORUS

Horus was a celebrated Egyptian god, the son of Osiris and Isis. He was a curious deity of many roles: a sky god, a hunter and warrior god, and a god of protection.

As a sky god Horus took the form of a falcon whose right eye was the sun and whose left eye was the moon. In a fierce battle, Horus' malicious uncle Seth in the form of a black boar wrenched out his moon eye and tore it to pieces. The moon god Thoth then searched in the dark for the lost eye, found the pieces and patched them together to make the Eye of Horus whole again. It thus acquired magic properties: it became the all-seeing eye of omniscience, keen to spot the slightest injustice. The Eye of Horus (or *wedjat*) can be bought, in ceramic or metal form, as an amulet. Buy one and keep it by you as an intense totem of the falcon's fearsome cosmic vision. Working with the Eye of Horus will align you with the Third Eye, the mystical eye of understanding, and give you the power of reflection and revelation.

BEYOND VISION

The hawk is a solar symbol of superiority, aspiration, spirit, light and liberty. When scanning a landscape, the keen-eyed hawk sees more than we do. Yet the medium of sight – light waves traveling to the retina – is the same for the bird as for us. When we look at a situation, the truths that we fail to perceive are there all the time – that we do not see them is attributable to our own imperfections of vision. Tune into your hawk companion, and see if you can travel to the realities that lie beyond what is immediately apparent.

CAT

FRIEND OF THE NIGHT

Magic and mystery – this is the cat. Cats see into the spirit world, hence they may hiss and spit at "nothing" in their reaction to beings that exist in other realms. They clearly see the unseen and they often protect humans from malevolent forces. Cats purr and send healing vibrations to their owners. During anxious, stressful times in your life, you would do well to pet a cat.

Lithe and silent, the cat comes and goes of its own accord. In its domestic incarnation there is a paradox: the creature appreciates affection, yet is strongly independent. We are fascinated by its wild instinct, but we are also wary of it – we know how instinct can suddenly surface with a snarl.

The black cat enjoys the perfect disguise as it slinks through the night, invisible but for its bright eyes. We, too, can move efficiently, without drawing attention to ourselves when the need arises. In Tai Chi, there is a posture that carries the name "Walk like a cat." An 18th-century Tai Chi text by Wang Tsung-Yueh describes how the upright body must be stable and comfortable, without tension or stiffness, to be able to cope with an attack from any of the eight directions. Gradually, the practitioner becomes more refined and graceful in his movements – he begins to walk like a cat.

The cat represents the gift of solitude, and the art of following your own path, without seeking or even attracting attention. Personal power is formidable and subtle. It is something that is carried into each waking moment – the depth of awareness, the silent observation. The shaman absorbs this ability into his own repertoire of spiritual skills.

The philosopher Ludwig Wittgenstein said, "If a lion could talk, we could not understand him." This is no doubt true of domestic cats as well. However, there is a shared borderland between human and feline experience, and in this realm meaningful, speechless communication is possible.

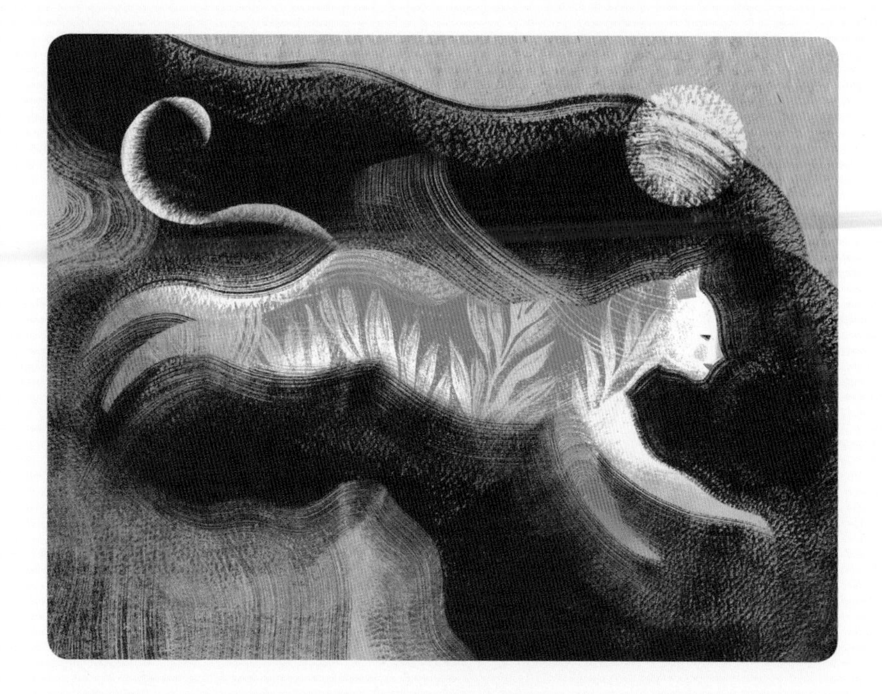

CAT WHISPERING

Cats offer a valuable way to extend your knowledge of animal powers – and by extension make acquaintance with your own feline spirit companion, the incarnation of the primordial stalker and hunter within ourselves. To develop empathy with a cat, follow these strategies:

Learn cat sounds These range from obvious ones such as the meow (which expresses need, but only to humans) and the purr (a sign of contentment) to the chatter, sometimes made before the pounce.

Learn the language of ears, tails and eyes Ears forward denotes contentment; ears back, anxiety; ears down, fear. Tail held high with a curl at the end expresses contentment; tail horizontal and swung from side to side, anger. Eyes wide open can signify aggression; a relaxed cat will close its eyes slightly, or even blink, to show that it fears no attack.

Communicate When talking to your cat, avoid staring at it directly – it will take this as a sign of aggression. While looking at its eyes, blink slowly to show that you are not hostile. Treat the animal as your equal.

MONKEY

THE ICONOCLAST

"If I am your spirit guide," jabbers the monkey appealingly, "I want you to have fun all the time. Play and laugh until it hurts. Promise me that, will you?"

Play is a powerful tonic for the soul and the trademark of the monkey is tomfoolery. Monkey takes a look at human behavior and says, "Stop being so serious!" Monkey is a show-off and a clown. What is it you most care about? Is it the priceless Ming Dynasty vase you bought at auction or that crystal punch bowl your grandmother left you? It does not matter what the item is or how much it is prized: monkey will make fun of your precious desires and all the beliefs you hold most dear. He shows us how to break all the rules of decorum and seriousness. Yet a monkey is no fool. Monkeys are crafty.

What does the monkey spirit tell us? Obviously, not to take ourselves too seriously. When you are experiencing difficult times, call on monkey energy to show you the lighter side of a situation. When we were children, we climbed on monkey bars to let out our frustrations. Find your adult monkey bars – it's a fact that physical exercise changes the chemistry of the brain and can help us deal with seemingly insoluble problems. Many Eastern forms of martial arts incorporate movements studied from animals. Moving the body in exercise can break a blocked energy pattern and help to bring new thinking to old issues.

Monkey teaches us to move, laugh, tumble and get up again running. This totem is sitting on the back of your chair howling at the vagaries of life that are having a negative effect on you. With monkey, you'll have to learn how to bend and stretch. Realizations can be painful with monkey. For example, it is not an entirely comfortable thought if we are told that education has an element of indoctrination in it. When monkey dashes your icons, he howls with amusement.

Animals have added much to the techniques and philosophy of the martial arts of the East. There are well-known movements such as tiger, leopard, snake, praying mantis and crane, but lesser known are the monkey forms. Long ago, Chinese Kung Fu master and monk Kau Sze was sent to prison. He wanted to escape, but the prison was surrounded by unusually fierce monkeys. He sought to find a way to defeat them by studying their activities through a small window in his cell. No two monkeys are alike – and Kau Sze came to realize how cunning, unpredictable and extraordinary these monkeys were. He practiced and trained in the thousands of deceptive movements and tricks of footwork he witnessed in the monkeys, and a lethal monkey Kung Fu was born.

Add to these battling combinations a couple of bottles of wine and you have the drunken monkey, a fighting style with seemingly uncontrolled movements that give the competent practitioner the appearance of being intoxicated. Suddenly, the drunken monkey strikes in a blaze of fury. Then, after the devastating blow, he jumps away and tumbles over and over.

It isn't usually a good idea to lose your control, but to relax your inner censor, the clamps of habit or fear that prevent you from being yourself, is often desirable. Between the frozen posture of the scared rabbit and the wild antics of the drunken monkey, there is a position to be struck. Learn from the drunken monkey, even if you do not approve of his anger.

PHOENIX

GOOD OUT OF BAD

There are phoenix legends from India, China, Greece, Egypt and Phoenicia (modern-day Lebanon and the coastal plains of Syria), among other lands. These legends tell of a mythical firebird that is promised immortality by the sun. After many centuries of life, the phoenix dies and is reborn from its own ashes.

In some legends, the phoenix is a mystic eagle representing the continuation of life in the flames of change. When the bird grows old, it flies into the sun and is destroyed. A worm is hatched from the bird's ashes, and the worm then becomes a great "sun eagle" rising from the flames.

In other legends this magical and gentle soul drinks only the morning dewdrops and represents the harmony of the heart with all that that implies. Good luck and good fortune, long life and happiness are symbolized by the phoenix. This beautiful creature represents fire and passion – the flame of true inspiration.

In virtually all mythologies, the bird symbolizes the power of transformation in response to hopelessness and devastation. "The phoenix, hope, can wing her way through the desert skies, and still defying fortune's spite, revive from ashes and rise," declared the famous 16th-century Spanish writer Miguel de Cervantes. This mythical being lifts us from the ashes of destruction into the blue skies of optimism and renewal. Faithfully making an appearance in times of trouble, this creature gives us new vision. The phoenix never dies – it perishes in flames, but from the red egg it lays atop the ashes it flutters anew, reborn.

In the worst of times, phoenix teaches us how to be victorious. Out of suffering, we grow in spirit. In heartbreak and sadness this bird sings an enchanting song that summons the forces of heaven.

Your Inner Flame

When you practice meditations devoted to the power of phoenix, face the south if you live in the northern hemisphere and north if you live in the southern hemisphere. It is important to face the direction of summer, which is the direction of the phoenix.

1. **First, prepare for your phoenix meditation by finding a red candle. Red is the color of fire and symbolizes the phoenix spirit within you. You may also like to wear red or orange clothing.**
2. **Find a quiet place where you can sit undisturbed. Take some time to relax and still your mind. Now open your eyes and focus your gaze on the candle flame.**
3. **Become aware of the flame that burns within you. In your mind's eye see a bright flame alive within the core of your being. It is a flame of hope and truth. Spend some minutes focused on its bright power of optimism and renewal.**
4. **Bring to your attention a problem that has been worrying you for some time. Expose your problem to the full power of your inner flame of hope and truth. Watch your problem burn away to ashes.**
5. **Close your meditation by thanking phoenix for her help and guidance.**

THE NOBLE FIRE BIRD

The word phuong *in Chinese means the male phoenix, which is solar and has yang energy. The female phoenix is called* huang *and she is yin and lunar. She is humble, peaceful, beautiful and delicate, while the male is bold, martial, assertive and combative. Appearing with the dragon, the symbol of the emperor, the phoenix is feminine and symbolizes the empress. Together they signify devotion, respect and the male and female aspects of imperial power. In imperial times only the empress could wear the symbol of the phoenix.*

JAGUAR

SHAPE-SHIFTING STALKER

The jaguar is one of the most mysterious animals on earth. It is the ruler of the night when phantoms and ancestral spirits stir in the deep forests. Night is the time of fantastic shapes and frightening sounds. But jaguar will not be seen because his disguises are numerous. Jaguar has the mental capability to shift into different forms at will. He may appear as a large rock, unmoving and inert, or he might be that dark shape in a tree that you are sure is a trick of the light.

The jaguar is strongly associated with shamanism because of his shape-shifting and stalking abilities and was sacred to the ancient Mayan people for this reason. Even though he is the ruler of the night, the unique "sunspots" on his fur allow jaguar to be equally comfortable in the daytime, blending invisibly into the sunlit jungle.

Shamans teach that to become a shape-shifter you must master energy. First, you must, by your very presence, learn to shift situations. This is done by subtle body adjustments and by mixing your vital force in a directed way into the apparent randomness of an event. But nothing is random and conditions are not created by pure chance. They are a flow of pre-existing events and energies. Like the jaguar, you can learn to break these patterns and stalk your prey.

If the spirit of the jaguar has captured your imagination, you may be involved in a situation that requires stealth. If you are normally outgoing and talkative, it could be time to shape-shift and become a quiet, introspective person. By changing your behavior in subtle ways, you will break the predictability of routine. This is a powerful mechanism, as it will allow you to see situations from entirely new vantage-points. Answers not previously found can be released from the creative unconscious by breaking out of the expected and taking a completely fresh approach.

According to the indigenous peoples of the Americas, the jaguar is a master of earth and sky, flying over the temple mounds of North and South America. Jaguar also journeys deep inside the earth over an ancient terrain of precise magnetic lines to energy points connecting the mounds in a great webbed complex. Jaguar is a solar being, a star traveler, carrying sunspots on its coat, and filled with the voice of the sun. The jaguar is the guardian and keeper of the great sun calendar of the Maya. Jaguar knows the will of the sun and passes the information over in dreams and visions to the shamans who have been trained to receive the message.

Join the elite class of Jaguar Knights by proceeding with alertness and courage through life, conscious of the majesty of the unpolluted self.

ELEPHANT

THE ALTRUISTS

Altruism is defined in the dictionary as unselfish concern, kindness, consideration for the welfare of others. In their attitude to the well-being of their families, elephants exemplify these wonderful qualities. Although elephants are the largest land animals on the planet, they take care of their young and elderly with great tenderness.

Elephants arrange their social behavior around tightly formed matriarchal groups. These groups consist of mothers, daughters, aunts, sisters and young elephants of both sexes. Adult males lead much more solitary lives. All of the females participate in rearing the younger elephants, providing protection and guidance. But there is usually one older matriarch that decides when the herd should migrate in search of food and water.

Elephants remind us of our own skills in caring for others and our power to protect and lead. Unlike many other animals, elephant is neither a stalker nor a predator in nature. Its power comes from its great size and its altruism. That this power is predominantly female is significant. Elephant speaks to us of the power of the feminine, the power that is present in caring for others, in protecting the weak and the small, in helping those who cannot manage for themselves. Elephant is the embodiment of the gentle giant.

We each have female and male power within us – yin and yang, or what Carl Jung termed the anima and the animus. When we are balanced physically, emotionally and spiritually, the female and male aspects within us operate in harmony. Elephant spirit calls upon us to exercise our powerful female traits. If this animal appears or appeals to you (whether you are a man or a woman), perhaps you are being called on to take care of your group or a person within your circle. Maybe you are being told to be their protector with a menacing display of trumpeting bravado. This is the elephant reminding you of your ancient instincts of altruism.

GANESHA, OVERCOMER OF OBSTACLES, LORD OF SUCCESS

Ganesha is one of the five most important Hindu deities. He has a roughly human form with the startling head of an elephant complete with large ears, trunk and curved tusks. Ganesha's big ears remind us that he listens when we call upon his powers. His head represents the soul and his body the illusions of life. His trunk is the carrier of the primal sound "om", the ancient sound of ultimate cosmic truth. He has a large pot belly, and crushes evil and destroys obstacles.

Many stories illustrate Ganesha's love of intelligence and learning – he is strongly associated with education, knowledge and wisdom, and also wealth. It is said that obstacles in the way of your spiritual or even material progress are easily brushed away when you call on Ganesha. He is often depicted riding on a mouse, which perhaps symbolizes the concept that if we work hard on the little things, the big issues will take care of themselves.

SPIDER

A WEB OF CONNECTION

Let spider help you spin a new fabric of being and make connections. Learn from the creativity of the spider and weave your life and personal space into a strong and beautiful pattern. Learn to be connected within the great web, to be like the spider and feel the psychic network all around you. Let your threads of gold and silver connect with and draw to you all that is important and necessary in your life.

Spiders are ancient masters of the great emptiness, and their way is the way of the web. They keep the emptiness together by weaving a multitude of connections. Spider tells us that all is linked and sends out purposeful strands with precise geometrical patterns.

Strands of the web transmit information, and what is far is brought near. Treading the web in spiraling motions, this creature masters the circularity of energy. The spider and her web are as one in the way that a lutanist becomes one with her instrument, the melody of the vibration conveying exactly what is caught in the web and what its condition is. The web is an extension of spider's whole being, the medium for crucial pulses of communication that tell of the wind, a leaf, or food.

Chief Seattle, leader of the Suquamish Native American tribe, understood the power of spider. He said in the mid-1880s, "Humankind has not woven the web of life. We are but one thread within it. Whatever we do to the web, we do to ourselves. All things are bound together. All things connect."

If spider is your spirit animal, connect with your web-building power. Cast your net wide and bring what you require to you. Listen to what vibrates your web by being in touch with the world. Spider teaches us to work in harmony with the energies of nature. Bathe in the sunshine. Let the wind caress you – your delicate web is tough and your silken filaments will hold firm.

A Spider Web Meditation

You can use this web meditation in many ways – for example, for health problems or to see how to become reconnected to the web of life.

1. Sit somewhere comfortable where you will not be disturbed. Take some deep breaths. Let any tension you may have fall from you. Take more deep breaths until you are centered, calm, peaceful and relaxed.
2. Imagine a small circle around you. This circle is yours and no one else's. Call the power of the Great Mysterious into your circle, which does not judge you, but just gives you unconditional love. Bask in that feeling.
3. Extend your circle out from your body and stay centered and relaxed. Now call down the powers of Spider Mother, the great weaver, to change your circle into a web. Let your circle fill in with a web, with you in the center.
4. Now name your web – for example, the web of relationships, the web of money or the web of spirit. It is your web – name it and claim it.
5. Examine your web using your medicine eye, your Third Eye. Look for any anomaly, anything caught in the web, any holes or problems with it.
6. Now you are going to mend your web. Ask what you have to do to repair the damage. Do you have to change your behavior? Do you have to challenge or accept things? Listen to the answer you receive and agree to act accordingly.
7. Close your meditation by thanking Spider Mother for her help.

SPIRIT AND DREAMCATCHERS

In some Native American cultures, spirit and dreamcatchers are used as sacred tools. Spirit catchers have a circular frame with a web made from twine tied to the frame, and are used on altars to catch good spirits and pass them through into this plane of existence to help us. Dreamcatchers have a strand of beads hanging from the center of the web to catch the good dreams that drip down the beads into the sleeper's dream world. You can put a small fetish of your spirit animal on your dreamcatcher to help you contact it when you are dreaming.

WOLF

TAMING THE WILDERNESS

Welcome to the wilderness, stretching far and away beyond our understanding. It is a natural, rough-and-tumble place, and can be as dangerous as a tiger about to pounce. Conversely, it can be a rosy dawn breaking over the gray shoulder of a mountain; as placid as a meandering river or as serene as a sacred oak grove.

The terrain in the wilderness is never boring. The paths are never straight in the land untamed, since the way of the wilderness is a crooked way. However, this wilderness is not the natural world. It is internal, dwelling within your own nature. This is the wilderness that cannot be tamed because it must remain wild so that you can be free. Seek and find a way to live with it. To do this, you need to recognize and honor the wilderness within your own being. Wolf can show you what to do, and guide you down unseen trails to your destination.

Wolf created civilization – wolves teach order in the face of chaos. At the beginning of the world, the Great Spirit sent the wolves out into the wilderness to measure the earth. They came back to the Great Mysterious One and told of what they had experienced and learned. Great Spirit said, "As you have named it, so shall it be." Wolves can clearly interpret and impart the way to others. Wolves can never be deceived because they watch and pay careful attention; they listen and see the signs. Knowing the trails and how to navigate them, they are never lost.

Wolves have dignity and courage in the face of adversity, and will do whatever a situation demands. They are steadfast and loyal, and will fight for their family or pack. Wolf is often called pathfinder. If you have been led astray and are confused and lost, ask wolf to show you the right path, to lead you through the maze of pitfalls and traps strewn in front of you. With wolf's help you can realign with your soul's purpose.

WILDERNESS GUIDE

Run with the wolves Let your spirit soar, dance, jump, play, roll around, bark, howl and yodel to the big moon.

Be at home in the wilderness Let your wolf companion lead you to hidden places that no one visits. You will find sources of renewal here – secret springs at the back of beyond.

Get organized Wolf teaches order. Sort out the things in your life that beg to be organized. Even wild animals need their own intuitive systems.

Lone wolf or running with the pack? Consider if the wolf pack is the right way for you, or whether you should be a lone wolf. Can you strike a happy balance between friends and family on the one hand and your own unique nature on the other?

Explore the power of twilight A period of transition and transformation, twilight is said to be the hour of the wolf, a time when the wolf spirit is strong. Native American elders claim that prayers made during twilight have immense power.

HOWLING WOLF

Wolves communicate in various ways, through body gestures, scent and tail position. Two wolf packs will draw attention to each other by howling, and their calls can mean trouble for the smaller group. Wolves will howl to strengthen communal bonds. Members of a wolf pack will howl at different tones and pitches, making it difficult for another pack to judge their numbers. Wolves were often called Big Mouth in Native America because they were believed to be able to deliver messages to the world beyond.

LION

ROYAL ENERGY OF THE SUN

If you are a person who likes to take charge, there is no better totem animal you can have than lion – it reigns supreme. Royal and stately, lion is an emblem of stability and sovereign power. While lionesses have no mane, the long, shaggy mane of the male lion is his defining feature. The lion's mane can be found in early artistic renderings and astrological iconography, in which it represents tendrils of the sun or solar rays, and therefore the energy expended by the sun.

Lions teach a calm and noble dignity. When necessary, they also teach courage and assertiveness. Lions tell you to have pride in your appearance and accentuate your strengths. Just as the lion's mane gives the male lion status, dignity and grandeur, your look and style can do the same for you.

Join your energy with that of the sun king. The lion and the sun are firmly tied together in many cultures and down through the ages both have been linked with kingship and royalty. In ancient Babylon, for example, the lion was a symbol of royalty, and Persian royalty was linked to the sun.

The Masai people have a lion-centered culture and men seek to manifest the powers of lion. They wear a headdress similar to a lion's mane and are armed only with a shield and a spear. A young man's rite of passage involved going out by himself to hunt the lion on the African savannah. Although for most of us the days of lion hunting are over, the symbiotic power shared by humans and lions is ever present. When you find and internalize this connection with the lion, your life will change for the better.

People with lion as their spirit animal can easily overcome stress by bringing themselves into alignment with lion's energy of strength and moral courage. If lion is your totem, face up to the issues and take the initiative. Meet challenges with your unquestionable will and your easy, natural nobility. Be open and content with who you are.

An Alchemical Meditation

This is a meditation on the lion of ancient alchemy. Alchemists sought to find the Philosopher's Stone, which would turn base metals into gold. In the Middle Ages this was transmuted into a mystical quest for closeness to the divine. Animals were used metaphorically to mark the different alchemical stages. The green lion devouring the sun symbolized the point at which the transformation into gold could first be seen.

1. Sit somewhere comfortable where you will not be disturbed. Become aware of your body. Breathe in harmony with an even rhythm. We begin our meditation by becoming the yellow lion, which in alchemy represents gold, but not gold as we usually think of it.
2. Bring a beautiful golden light from your feet upward and feel its warming qualities. Bring this light all the way to the top of your head. Bathe in the golden light of the ancient philosophers. Feel the light of the yellow lion purifying you into the perfect human. Gold according to the ancient Vedic teachings represents immortality. Claim this quality for yourself.
3. Next, call upon the powers of the green lion who devours the sun. Call in a beautiful green light, filling your body with perfect green all the way up to the crown of your head. Feel the healing powers of the color green, the light that purifies matter. Let the loving, embracing green light eat all impurities and everything toxic. Become purified.
4. Now call the red lion of alchemy. Bring the focused red light into your body, filling you with a ruby red light spangled with flecks of gold. Let the red light fill you with spiritual passion and raw energy. These flecks of gold represent a search for universal truth within the material world. With truth you can harness the power of an awakened inner sun, the philosopher's stone, the jewel more precious than gold.
5. Close your meditation by thanking the green and red lions for their wisdom, strength and understanding.

GRIZZLY BEAR

FEARLESS HEART

The grizzly bear is greatly venerated in shamanic cultures, embodying a strong will and determination. Grizzlies are considered to have supernatural abilities and to be visionaries and healers. They are also brave, having the power of the warrior and a fearless heart. In Chinese alchemy, the bear is the symbol of potency and masculinity. Generally, grizzlies are solitary animals. However, they will congregate near streams, lakes and rivers during salmon spawning when they feed on the bountiful fish supply.

With a valiant nature, the grizzly brings daring and courage into the world. Sometimes, blustering is cowardly, being brave only in the sense of displaying bravado based on fear. Shaking and quivering, we face our enemy, but we cover our fear with a mask of courage. This is never the case with grizzly – he is truly fearless and centered, and is never afraid to strike.

Unlike smaller bears, the grizzly can't escape danger by climbing trees. Therefore, if a grizzly feels under threat he will stand his ground, rising on his hind legs to reach 8–9ft (2.5–2.75m), his fierce eyes and large head challenging, his arms menacing and brandishing long-clawed paws. How astounding and terrifying! However, generally bears avoid human contact and very rarely view humans as prey. Human attacks tend to occur when the bear has been surprised at close range or is defending young.

A wise man said that action is the best quality to overcome fear. The grizzly bear knows this and is never hesitant to act. This is because action produces change. Conditions alter in tune with the grizzly's brave heart.

In Native America, grizzly bears are said to be our closest relatives. They are the most powerful shamans, nurturing and loving yet fierce and protective. If grizzly bear is your spirit animal, familiarize yourself with some of its powers, and you too will discover that you have a fearless heart.

THE GRIZZLY SHAMAN

There is a great deal of lore and legend surrounding grizzlies – the bear has been mythologized into almost god-like proportions. In Native America, the grizzly bear is the left-handed one, the shaman, the tracer, the tracker, the warrior, the healer and the thief, and possesses many supernatural and magical qualities.

There is no more powerful healer than a grizzly bear shaman. If you were to enter his cave you would find a ceremonial space surrounded by torches that throw orange light over the expanse. On a rock shelf are herbs and roots and healing preparations. On the floor is a musty grizzly bear robe with the bear's head still attached, tossed over a bed of branches and moss. There are sage and tobacco twists surrounding the robe. You are given a large can of bitter honey and a bucket of water with a dipper. This, you are told, is your nourishment for the next several days. You are told to dream and left to your own devices.

After a while, a grizzly shaman enters the cave on all fours, grunting and snorting. Could it be a real grizzly? Could the animal be coming to sample your honey? No, it is a man, but his presence is more like a bear. He nuzzles over you, grumbling and snorting. You feel a primordial force from this shaman. He fumigates you with a smouldering piece of osha root. He sings, dances and blows tobacco smoke over you. It is somehow reassuring. He tells you to sleep, to dream, and leaves the cave snorting as he goes.

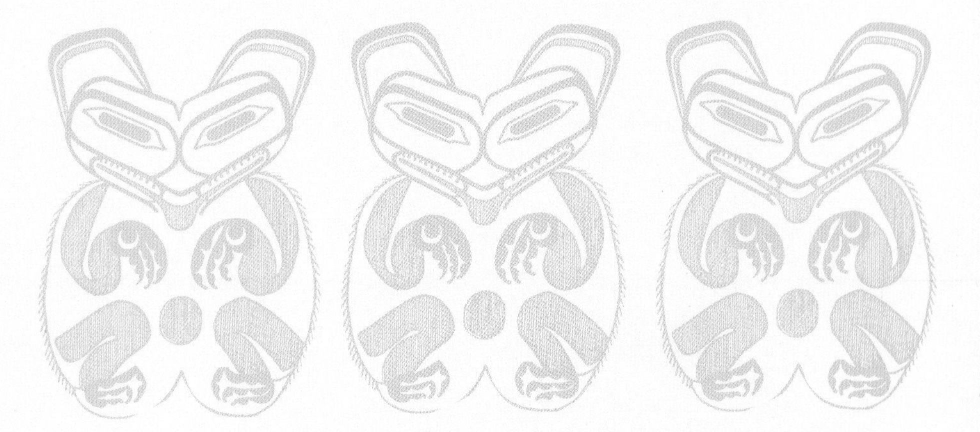

CROW AND RAVEN

THE VOID

"If men had wings and bore black feathers, few of them would be clever enough to be crows." So said the Reverend Henry Ward Beecher, the 19th-century social reformer. These birds are powerful spirit animals, and you may consider yourself fortunate if either one or both are your totem.

Crows and ravens often live long lives. It is said that these lovers of shiny objects are able to see death. The handsome blue-black birds are found all over the world. True crows are recognized by their long black wings, and both crow and raven are strong-beaked. Crafty and cunning, they possess extraordinary mental powers and are also loud and raucous.

Crow and raven represent the cosmic void, the black emptiness of the universe. Many traditions hold that crow and raven flew out of that emptiness and into the everyday reality we understand. Let crow and raven carry you into and out of that dark matrix, in the process helping you gain greater awareness of this profound truth about the nature of reality.

When you feel you are in darkness, ask for crow and raven to give you a sign as to which way to go. Indigenous people have said that a crow is a transmitter of messages, signs and sometimes warnings. A raven has been said to be an omen – a kind of message, but usually of heavy, dramatic portent. In Celtic mythology the great warrior queen Morrigan, who was associated with prophecy and death, sometimes appeared in the form of a crow, flying above warriors at the scene of a battle.

Let crow and raven be your guides through the dark labyrinths. Both crow and raven are at home in the confusion that is life. Although they are thieves and tricksters by nature, they teach right behavior by bringing clues and communications. If a crow flies overhead and gives you a series of loud strong calls, it would be best to heed these calls and become alert and aware. Some tribal people maintain that crow and raven brought life itself into this world when they brought human souls from the primordial darkness into the light.

In various mythologies of Asia and North Africa, the crow was associated with the sun; in some traditions it was actually believed to inhabit the sun, thus illustrating the light-bringing quality of this bird. Some Native American tribes maintain that it was the cunning and bold raven and his cousin the crow that brought light on the tips of their wings into our world from the inside of an eternal night.

Let these mysterious birds bring light to any situations in your life that are mired in darkness, confusion or despair. They are powerful spirits to connect with as your totem, yet they can represent many different meanings, so interpretations should be carefully considered. For example, raven is not always an omen of darkness: it can represent shadow or the soul. Crow can also be a trickster, leading you on a search for shiny treasure. Whatever role crow or raven come to play in your life, one thing is certain: it is bound to be illuminating.

TWO RAVENS: THOUGHT AND MEMORY

Odin, the chief god of the Norse, a bloodthirsty warrior who relished carnage in battle, had two ravens, Thought (Huginn) and Memory (Muninn), which each perched on one of his shoulders. They scouted the earth in reconnaissance for Odin on a daily basis, and reported back to him, giving him news by whispering into his ears.

Thought and Memory may have different tales to tell, because Memory may be inaccurate, or limited, or distorted by strong emotions. Be like Odin when assessing the lessons of what happens: listen to Thought as well as to Memory.

GORILLA

MIGHTY STRENGTH

There are legends in Central Africa that the sagging sky is held up at the cardinal points by four Herculean gorillas. They watch with broken hearts the destruction of their kin, and when the gorilla tribes have vanished, the gorillas will let go of the sky. It is said that our entire world will then be destroyed.

Coming upon a 5ft 9in (1.75m), 300 lb (135kg) adult male silverback mountain gorilla in the Virungan Mountains of Rwanda must be a sobering experience. Such an event could certainly have inspired imaginations wild enough to create *King Kong*. Rarely, since the dinosaurs, has an animal inspired such fear and awe in humans. But why? After all, humans and apes – including gorillas – share 98 percent of the same DNA structure.

Why do humans have such an innate fear of one of our closest primate relatives? It is certainly true that gorillas are among the strongest creatures on earth. There are tales from the early part of the 20th century of gorillas being shipped to countries around the world for display in freak shows. Because of his uncommon strength, Gargantua, one early victim of this morbid curiosity, could bend large rubber tyres like an accordion with his hands. Gorillas were prized for their strength and ferocity, and in the early 1920s and '30s people flocked to see these "savage" beasts behind bars.

But the savagery of gorillas was grossly overstated. They are, in fact, herbivores living in highly social groups of related animals that care for their young until they are three years old. Fully-grown adult males, or silverbacks, will even care for orphaned young if they come upon them in the forest – hardly savage behavior.

The application of gorilla spirit in our lives involves the use of quiet strength. Appearing to threaten can be more effective and powerful than actually threatening. There are times in life when your safety will be questioned, either by real forces or imagined ones. Gorillas beat their large, flat chests during these times, the sound and gesture presenting a fear-provoking display to an aggressor, as if the gorilla's actual size and strength were not enough.

Gorilla is a wonderful spirit animal – retiring, quiet and mighty. Gorilla power helps us to acquire a patient strength and determination. It teaches us that there are times when we have to beat our chests and stand up to the bully in the playground, whether that bully is real or part of the negative imaging in our heads. Gorilla energy walks with serious purpose and strength. The silverback uses but a small percentage of the actual available force to protect his troop and intimidate its foes. The gorilla totem is powerful symbolic energy. This spirit animal can help us overcome the mental foes that prey on us. Shake your gorilla fist at the doubts and fears plaguing you and watch them run for the jungle.

Gorilla habitats are dwindling and the threats to gorillas from poachers and human territorial expansion are very real – there are probably fewer than 1,000 wild mountain gorillas left in the world today.

BEFRIENDING THE SILVERBACK

A silverback is an adult male gorilla, so-called because of the patch of silver hair on his back. These animals are powerful leaders, each having a troop of followers – between five and thirty in number. The role of the silverback is to adjudicate over disagreements, decide on the group's movements, and generally be in charge of every individual's safety and well-being.

You may have a silverback in your life – a dominant, decisive person who believes that he or she has to the right to lead. There is no point in trying to topple a silverback in conflict. Instead, summon up a spirit animal with subtle intuitive powers – perhaps a bear, or a dolphin, or even a hummingbird. Show the silverback what you can do in the guise of this very different creature. Incongruous pairings can be invincible together.

CROCODILE

QUEEN OF THE NILE

Crocodiles are skilled. These reptiles are cold-blooded killers with the patience to be still and wait. When a victim is near, they dart to the attack, and are extremely fast. The Nile crocodile has a highly developed brain, more so than any other reptile. Both its hearing and eyesight are good, and it also has an excellent sense of smell.

In Egyptian cosmology, Sobek, the crocodile god, emerged from the waters of chaos to create the world. Crocodiles have a rich history of myth and symbol. They were believed to bring the rains upon which the fertility of the Nile Valley depended; yet at the same time they were feared as agents of death. Hence these powerful creatures had both positive and very negative associations.

Humans have a dread of encountering this creature, and rightly so. The Nile crocodile is one of the largest of the crocodile family. Animals such as wild dogs, jackals and gazelle, drawn down to the water for a cool drink, are the usual feast of the crocodile. Swiftly and ferociously, this formidable creature seizes its unfortunate victim, holding it under water until it drowns.

Crocodiles are amongst the most ancient of creatures. The disturbing cry of the crocodile is antediluvian, and catapults us back in time. It harks back to the age of reptiles and forward through the successions of pharaohs to our present days – an immense stretch of time.

Egypt has been blessed by the Nile River, aptly called "the river of life". The White Nile is arguably the longest river in the world and Egypt lays claim to some 22 percent of its length. The yearly inundation or flood enriches the land, making it fertile and bountiful. One of the oldest civilizations sprang up in the valley on either side of the river. On sandbars and riverbanks motionless crocodiles sunbathe. Crocodile is the watcher, the guardian, the keeper of time, and is truly the queen of the Nile.

A Crocodile Bath

This exercise can help you tap into the tremendous power of crocodile, the power of patience, survival and knowledge stretching back through eons of time. It is designed for women only.

1 Run comfortably warm water in a large tub. Enter the water slowly with your stomach facing down, stretch out and relax.

2 Stretch out your arms with your elbows opposite one another to form a diamond shape in front of you and lay your head on your hands. Rest comfortably with your head out of the water on the rim of the tub. The heels of your feet should be touching, with toes pointing outward. Close your eyes and relax.

3 In this semi-floating position, call the spirit of the crocodile. Feel yourself submerged in different levels of reality, slipping between two worlds, inner and outer. Feel yourself gliding through other universes, realities and dimensions. Take long, deep breaths and release them easily and comfortably, feeling the crocodile spirit. Do this for as long as you are comfortable. When you are finished, thank the crocodile spirit. Roll onto your back, rest awhile and continue with your queenly bath.

BUFFALO

THE ART OF GIVING

The American bison, better known as the buffalo, is the largest native animal of North America, found only on that continent. These mighty animals migrated across the great plains in enormous herds of many thousands – once there were millions of buffalo. There are reports that describe how bands of buffalo were seen stretching as far as the eye could see, the dust rising with the sound of tattooing hoofs and bellowing wails.

In the spring and summer, the buffalo feeds on lush grasses and other vegetation. In the fall and winter, its diet is narrowed and hunger drives the animal. In the winter, it ploughs the snow with its nose until it is torn and bleeding in order to reach the sparse grass underneath.

On the prairies, the lives of the buffalo and of the tribal people were entwined. Gifts from the buffalo included the hide coverings of the tipis, moccasins, bedding, tough membranes for war shields and clothing made from buffalo skin. In fact, the buffalo furnished almost every necessity of life, and was the spiritual center of the people. The buffalo symbolized the art of giving.

You would not think of the buffalo as a timid creature. Yet in fact these animals are easily spooked and an entire herd can take off in a panic at the slightest likelihood of danger. Long ago, before the horse and rifle, the people of the prairies would fan out on foot, make a lot of noise and stampede the animals to a "buffalo jump" over a cliff edge, where they fell to their death. First, there was a ceremony in which the people said prayers and sang songs of gratitude and thanksgiving, then the butchering began. The fat, tongue and kidney of the buffalo were particularly valued. The meat was hung on poles in the sun to dry and then stored for the long winter. Every part of the buffalo was utilized.

For various historical reasons, the buffalo were hunted to near extinction. The extermination of the buffalo changed the way of Native American life for ever. In many ways, the life of the prairie people was a reflection of the sacred buffalo's bounty – food, shelter and clothing. And to this was added the spiritual teachings of the buffalo – prayer, sharing, self-denial, altruistic self-sacrifice. Truly, the buffalo nations were masters of the art of giving, and the buffalo's teachings go to the very marrow of life. The buffalo gave their all. In difficult economic times, modern people can look to the buffalo and learn their lesson of sharing and generosity.

Tales linger on about the beloved buffalo and the great hunts. When food was scarce and the people were starving, there were gifted shamans with hunting power and the ability to call buffalo through ritual and charms. The shaman went out in the prairie and placed a buffalo skull facing east. Around his neck was a buffalo horn suspended on a braided buffalo-hair cord. He sang songs to enchant the buffalo and then raised the sacred pipe to the four corners of the earth, smoked the pipe and placed it in the skull. If all was done correctly, the buffalo heard and knew of the people's suffering. The buffalo came to give of themselves and were killed – a gift to the people.

THE RHYTHM OF HOOFBEATS

Throughout East Asia the buffalo was revered as one of humankind's most important helpers. Lao Tzu (570–490BC), the founder of Taoism, rode a buffalo as he journeyed to leave the disintegrating kingdom. When he arrived at the Han Gu Pass on the western border, the guard, realizing that Lao Tzu was leaving for good, asked him to write down the fruits of his wisdom to preserve them for the people. So Lao Tzu dismounted from the buffalo and wrote the Tao te Ching.

The rhythmic motion of a buffalo helps to rest our thoughts and prime our creativity. Before you begin a creative enterprise, imagine yourself on a buffalo, riding through the Asian countryside. When you feel ready, climb down from your buffalo and launch yourself into your project.

DRAGON
HIDDEN POWERS

The dragon is a charged mythological animal symbol. Creatures of mystery, dragons appear in many cultures across the globe with different associations and meanings. Seemingly, dragons are a mix of many extant animals such as alligators, lizards and snakes, as well as extinct ones such as the pterodactyl, a prehistoric flying reptile.

In Asia, dragons generally resemble snakes, whereas the European dragon has wings and breathes fire. There are other cultural differences too – Asian dragons are generally seen as primal forces of nature and are considered to possess great wisdom and have supernatural abilities. By contrast, the European dragon was generally a symbol of evil, a dangerous beast to be slaughtered, most famously in the legend of St George.

It is fascinating that dragon-like creatures have emerged in unrelated cultures all over the world. One theory is that the features of dragons – snake-like body, cat-like claws and the ability to fly like a bird of prey – embody the three types of animals all humans would have most cause to fear. Others have speculated that dragons have been inspired by the remains of dinosaurs found around the world. Others still believe that dragons are alive and well, and operate deep within us at a spiritual level. Sometimes powerful dragon energy surfaces and causes trouble; at other times it has the opposite effect of giving us extraordinary powers – powers we did not realize that we had.

When dragon awakens inside us, we are where we are supposed to be: the see-saw of time comes into perfect balance because we have tapped into a universal and ancient force. A thinker becomes a larger self, as if thinking thoughts from the center of the cosmos. It is as though dragon has flown us to the highest level of being, or that the dragon within us has married the entire universe.

BEOWULF AND GRENDEL

In the epic Anglo-Saxon poem and early adventure story *Beowulf,* the hero battles with Grendel, a fierce monster that has been killing the local people. Beowulf says to King Hroogar of Denmark, "They say you have a monster here. They say your lands are cursed. I am Beowulf and I'm here to kill your monster." Though the exact nature of the evil antagonist Grendel is not clear, this monster fits the archetype of the dragon very well, with scales, horny growths and blood-caked claws. Beowulf slays the malicious beast and then, at the bottom of the sea, he fights Grendel's mother in a close match, finally beheading her.

There are many similar dragon legends which tell us that the power of dragon is great indeed, a power that we can learn to control and harness for ourselves. In the legend of St George and the dragon, St George rescues a princess from the dragon by transfixing the dragon with his spear and then leads him, completely tamed, by the princess's girdle.

CHAPTER 3

Inner Wisdom

When you engage with an animal spirit you awaken new perceptions. An animal, or indeed any phenomenon of nature, is intrinsically mysterious. What is inexpressible about another life-form connects with the biggest questions about existence. How and why did the cosmos come into being? Why is there something rather than nothing (as philosophers often put it)? Meditation can give us a wordless awareness of the truths that lie behind these conundrums. When we gaze into the eyes of another creature, we are confronted with profound mysteries, of which the animal is a living embodiment.

This chapter introduces animals that can lead us to new insights and new awareness. If we are willing to open our minds and listen, we can grow in spiritual maturity and make progress on our inner journey.

DOG

GUARDIAN OF THE LAW

The dog tribe is vast, embracing all domesticated dogs, foxes, wolves, coyotes and even jackals. It is reckoned that approximately 12,000 years ago dogs were domesticated from a wolf ancestor, and they have remained our faithful companions ever since. According to the stories of the Tehuelche Indian people, the dog was created by the Sun God to keep the first man and woman company, and throughout the ancient world dogs were so loved that they were often interred with their owners in tombs. Science has confirmed what many people instinctively know – people who own dogs lead less stressful lives and live longer. Close companionship with a dog can often heal a traumatic experience.

Dogs were vital for helping humans hunt game and track their way through the wilderness. In the same way, in many myths, dogs also guided people in the afterlife. In ancient Egypt the god of the dead, Anubis, had the head of a jackal; while according to Greek mythology, the three-headed dog Cerberus guarded the gates of the underworld.

Dogs are wonderful moral guardians: they sense when we have left the way of integrity and justice. Dogs have much to say about such lapses – they mope around in distress and encourage us to get back on our proper path. Dogs have a nose for falseness, and keep away from people who they feel are bogus. And when their masters are unfairly treated, dogs know it.

With dog as your totem animal you can expect to uncover great reserves of loyalty and devotion. Undivided attention and love is where dog energy is centered; this animal can guide you back to the path of faith and love. Strongly grounded in the home, dog is nevertheless a wonderful companion through the mysteries of the wilds and the unknown. Dog will walk strange paths with you, affirming that if you want to seek adventure, he or she will be there at your side.

TALES OF LOYALTY

Xanthippus was the father of Pericles, the famous statesman of ancient Athens. He was a war hero from the time of the invasion of the Persians, and in the early stages of the conflict he commanded the Athenian navy. History books tell us that in 480BC the Greeks were forced to leave Athens and sail away to escape Persian despotism. The animals knew that they were leaving, and the dogs howled, sending up a dreadful racket.

When the ships sailed, one dog leapt into the sea and swam alongside the vessel until it reached the island of Salamis. Exhausted but happily reunited with his owner Xanthippus, the dog died. The people gave this heroic canine the solemn burying rites reserved for humans. Now, more than two millennia later, the ground surrounding the place where the dog was interred is called "the hound's burying place".

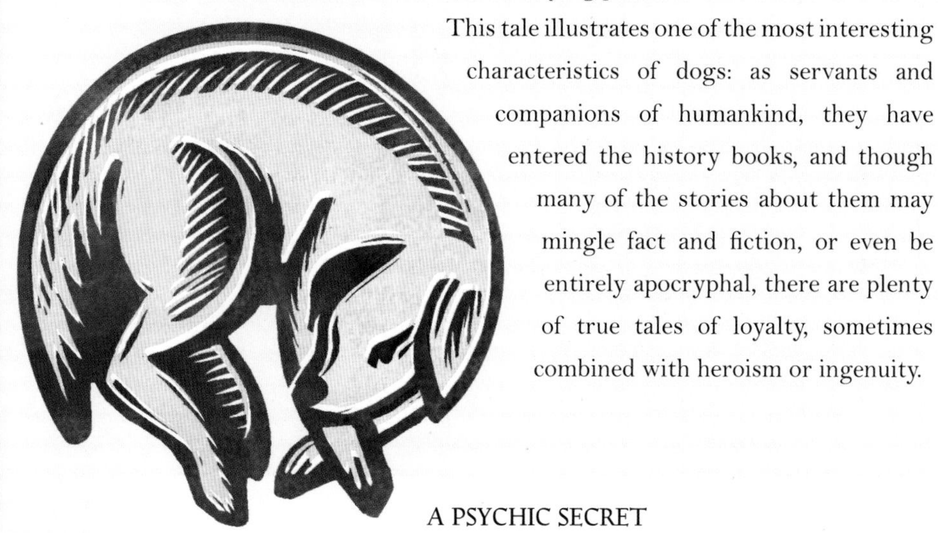

This tale illustrates one of the most interesting characteristics of dogs: as servants and companions of humankind, they have entered the history books, and though many of the stories about them may mingle fact and fiction, or even be entirely apocryphal, there are plenty of true tales of loyalty, sometimes combined with heroism or ingenuity.

A PSYCHIC SECRET

Smell is a dog's primary sense. Metaphysically, the sense of smell is related to intuition. If you have a problem, try "sniffing out" the answer instead of relying on logic. Many intuitives pay attention to their sense of smell when they are doing psychic readings. You can do the same. Get comfortable, direct your sense of smell into the Third Eye region of your mind, which deals with intuitive revelation, and ask how to solve your difficulties.

HORSE

NATURAL NOBILITY

Horses have been honored as creatures of majesty and power for thousands of years. There are cave paintings of horses in Spain and France dating back 15,000 years or more. Horses keep company with shamans, and there is a close connection between the two. Some maintain that a shaman's drum can change magically into a horse (see page 11); others say that shamans keep magical horses contained in gourds. These genie-like spirit animals have the power of seeing into the future, and they protect the shamans from danger.

There is nothing so fine or noble as a beautiful, spirited horse. According to the ancient inhabitants of the Altai Mountains in Central Asia the universe itself was a horse – the great horse of compassion. His head was the dawn of the sky. The Morning Star was his left eye and the Evening Star his right eye. His hide held the moon, stars and planets, space was inside his stomach and his body was time. The four winds were contained in his breath and under him was our earth. We humans were the intermediate ones seeking understanding of this great horse.

In many cultures around the world the white horse has a special spiritual significance. The ancient sacred Indian texts, the Vedas, describe how in the final incarnation of Vishnu as the savior of the world, the great lord either will appear riding a white horse or will take the form of a white horse. White horses were sacrificed in the ancient Vedic rite of *Ashvameda,* and a similar sacrifice was practiced by the Hungarian Magyars. Two of the most important Christian saints, James and George, traditionally ride pure white horses, while other cultures describe white horses pulling the chariot of the sun across the sky.

Native Americans were the finest of horse people. The Comanche, a tribe noted for its skill with horses, were able to carry out raids deep into Mexico. On the plains, the horse brought a new legacy of cultural expansion. With horses, Native Americans could hunt more effectively and move more goods quicker than ever before. Horses also allowed people the mobility to relocate tribal villages many miles away. Horses prevented Spanish and white expansionism into the American southwest for two centuries.

With horse as your totem you have the energy of speed, nobility and grace. You have innate strength, dignity and beauty.

Meditations on the Horse

1 **You must first become centered, either standing up or lying down. Feel the energy of a horse. Give yourself permission to bring in the energy, the spirit, the very soul of a horse.**

2 **Let go of any separation you may feel and become one with this animal. In your mind's eye, let go of any repression or hesitation and become free – free to walk slowly into a lush green pasture. Feel the wind dancing in your mane.**

3 **You walk a little faster now with joy and pride. Feel the drumming of your hooves on the ground. Romp, kick and trot. Rear up on hind legs and paw the air with your hooves.**

4 **Now, like the wind you can dare to gallop fast and free. Your breath takes in the prairie-perfumed air, your nostrils flare. You are a wild horse at one with the wilderness.**

EAGLE

CLARITY OF VISION

According to some Native Americans, when the eagle calls from above it is the Great Spirit acknowledging you. This extraordinary creature is a member of the Accipitridae family, which includes osprey and all the hawks, and is the sovereign of birds. Shamans all over the world have courted the eagle for its powers and it is said that eagles were the first shamans. The eagle attains the highest spiritual states and is the greatest of warriors. Many cultures have viewed the eagle as a supernatural being. For example, in Hindu traditions the powerful creature Garuda had the body of a human and the head of an eagle and was the favored mount of Lord Vishnu, while in Greek mythology a giant golden eagle served as Zeus' messenger.

With its broad wingspan and muscular power, the eagle in flight is a magnificent sight. It swoops in broad, graceful curves, spiraling upward at each turn and ascending to altitudes where it is barely visible to the human eye. Yet from this vantage point it charts the ground below and hurtles rapidly downward to take any prey it desires.

Eagles have acute eyesight, in fact the most powerful in the animal kingdom – they can see six to eight times farther than most humans. Renowned for their visionary powers, they see directly ahead in addition to being able to view vast territories at either side. Having such accurate sight, eagles are able to teach clarity of vision, and if we have such clarity we can effectively gauge any situation.

The eagle is strong and fast and does not hesitate to do what is needed. With its sense of balance, it can put our troubles in perspective. How often do you stop to think of others less fortunate than yourself? Eagle brings warmth of heart and spiritual renewal, and its clarity of vision enables us to see by the true light.

An Eagle-Sun Meditation

Eagle power was said to be one of the greatest because it came from the "above-place". The eagle flies close to the sun and its power was thought to be held in consort with the sun and the heat and light it emanates. With the power of the "eagle-sun", the shaman could perform many magical acts.

Try to practice this meditation outside in the sunshine when there are blue skies overhead.

1. **Begin by stretching out your arms like someone on a high wire and move them slowly to steady your balance. Close your eyes.**
2. **Breathe in deeply and evenly, and let your arms gradually become wings as you feel the feathers sprouting. Let your wings catch the wind and with each slight movement buoy you up. Join with the spirit of eagle. Feel yourself soar gracefully into the heavens.**
3. **Imagine that you are making large circles in the air and relish the power of flight. Rise on the thermal currents. Feel the warming rays of the sun, blessing and caressing you. Let the wind sing and your sharp eyes take in the world below. Feel sustained by the light of the sun and the song of the wind. Feel nourished by the sun – and at peace.**
4. **When you are ready, float back slowly into your body and give thanks for the experience.**

EAGLE BONE WHISTLES

Eagle bone whistles, made from the long wing bone of an eagle, are used in various Native American ceremonies, including the Sundance. The whistles make an eerie high-pitched sound like the cry of an eagle. This repetitive "eagle cry" is said to be pleasing to the ancestor spirits. The whistle hangs from a rawhide necklace, usually with an eagle plume attached. This plume in itself is a teaching. When powerful forces are coming at you, become like an eagle plume – light of spirit – and waft above them.

POLAR BEAR
HEALING THE PLANET

In the harsh northland of ice and snow, during the sunless winters, the people huddled in their igloos and told stories of great hunters, and magical foxes, caribou and seals. They spoke of heroic deeds and of confrontation with supernatural animals, and of how the ice bears are linked to the healing of the planet.

They told how the polar bear spoke to the shamans of indigenous peoples and to mystics everywhere throughout the world. For the peoples of the Arctic this bear was vital for every aspect of their culture. The fur was used for trousers and shoes, the gallbladder and heart were used for medicine and the teeth were worn as potent talismans. But beyond that the bear had mystical significance. Earth and human health are interconnected. Healing the planet, bear teaches, is about healing yourself. This increases harmony and good energy everywhere. Through dreams, the polar bear reverses negativity and destruction, and moves the earth itself into a healing mode.

Polar bears are as white as the snow of their environment – the icebergs, ice mountains and the frozen steppes of the far north. The bears are good at swimming, hunting and fishing. They dive deep into the icy waters and surface with a salmon in their mouths, and they swim underwater like stealthy submarines. Seals are one of their favorite foods; they lie in wait on the ice for them, the bear using its excellent sense of smell to locate a seal breathing hole. As soon as the seal surfaces for air, the bear attacks.

There was a time, it is told, when polar bears were human. During the day they would take off their great white coats and become people. At night, they would come home, put on their coats and change back into polar bears. Those bears taught us that we are actually animals. We can go out in the world and do what humans do, but sometimes we must return home, put on our animal skin and go forth with strength and courage.

A Northern Lights Meditation

Sit comfortably in a quiet place, close your eyes and let the polar bear become the focus of your meditation.

1 **Imagine yourself in the north on the very roof of the world. The Northern Lights flicker and streak across the backlit gray sky, tossing bouquets of color – a soundless festival of shimmering lights. Light blades of yellow, green, orange and purple flare above the drifts of white virgin snow. It is icy cold, but your thick, white, ice-encrusted fur keeps you snug and warm. There is a cold blue steam coming from your nostrils. This is an uninhabitable glacial land for most, but not for you. You exist and survive here in the vast reaches of snow and ice. You stand transfixed, taking in the beautiful sight in front of you while the crystalline snow gives off ghosts of refracted brilliant light. And above, there is an ocean of many-colored icy fires.**

2 **Now begin to gather the rainbows of light and make them into a ball in your white fists with long black claws. Draw this ball to your chest. It is a brilliant sphere full of loving peace. Imagine that you can send the ball anywhere you want – you can. Send the ball to any person or place that needs healing. Continue sending out this healing energy for several minutes.**

3 **Once you have finished your meditation, move back to yourself gradually. Gently reabsorb the loving, healing, peaceful energy into your chest. Become aware of your immediate surroundings and, when you are ready, open your eyes.**

COYOTE

CRISIS MANAGEMENT

Legend tells us that coyote brought the world into being by singing the first song, the creation song. Unfortunately, he was just learning to sing and so hit some very harsh notes. Thus we have many bumps on the road of life, all thanks to coyote.

People have been trying to exterminate the scavenger and hunter coyote for a very long time, but they have failed because he is a survivor. Coyotes are found in urban areas such as Beverly Hills, as well as in the Arctic north and as far south as southern Mexico. Coyote is an opportunistic hunter and will change his hunting style to suit the conditions. He can hunt in packs, baiting and harassing larger animals such as deer to the point of exhaustion. But he may also stalk small prey alone, like a cat. He may scavenge garbage sites and carrion, yet he will also eat fruit and vegetables – coyote is a highly adaptable animal.

Native American traditions teach that just at the point when you think your life is in good order, coyote will appear and trip you up – you'll find yourself in the clutches of the master trickster. Coyote has charisma and charm – but beware, he is also a hustler and a con artist. On account of your new friend, the coyote, things quickly unravel and fall apart. Coyote teaches you to get your life back under control and take charge, being wary of tricks and setbacks along the way.

In one Native American creation story, First Mother was patiently placing the stars up in the night sky in orderly rows. Coyote watched and couldn't bear to see such neatness and order. When First Mother left, he hurried over and jerked with all his might the blanket that held all the stars. The stars flew up helter-skelter in a random mess. That is the nature of the coyote – bringing confusion into the world. Is this what has happened to you? Take heed and bring your world back into order.

The Coyote "Ha Ha" Mantra

We can learn from the clever tricks of the coyote. This exercise emphasizes the laughter and support you can gain from the teasing, clever and adaptable coyote pack.

1 Gather six friends together and make a circle outside, preferably at night.

2 Each person in the circle must loudly say the word "ha!"

3 Let the word be howled around the circle until someone changes the word to "h" plus a different vowel – choose any one of "he", "hi", "ho" and "hu", the latter pronounced like the owl word, "woooooooo".

4 Howl a word twice ("he he"), then howl a word three times ('hu hu hu"), then afterward howl words in any combination, any number of times. Do not laugh; you are drawing on the playful, teasing trickster spirit.

5 Close by thanking coyote for the lessons you have learned.

SALAMANDER

SOULFUL ALCHEMY

The shaman performs a kind of primordial alchemy – releasing a transformative spirit from base matter. It is a fundamental principle of advanced modern thinking about mind, body and spirit that we all have within ourselves the resources we need to make important changes in our lives – that is, to find our destiny. Apart from the phoenix and the butterfly (see pages 58 and 96), no creature so powerfully suggests inner transformation as the salamander. It denotes the believer who resists the flames of temptation.

The heat of temptation burns within all of us, and so there is no reason to feel guilty about our appetites anymore than feeling guilty about the heat of our blood. By thinking of yourself as a salamander, you can freeze-frame the moment of temptation and choose to resist rather than succumb. And with the salamander as your spirit companion, resistance comes to be seen as a natural process rather than a stone wall erected against nature.

The appearance of the salamander heralds a time of change that is coming from sources outside the self. The salamander is a fiery element that roams between earth and water, and those people who have it as their totem often lead double lives. Salamander is the keeper of dreams, and its ability to live in water and on land demonstrates that dreaming can be lucid and connected to the earth mysteries. It can cloak itself in the face of adversity and is a magical talisman that brings comfort in the darkness.

Fighting Inner Fires

This meditation is designed to halt the appetites in their tracks, when to follow them would inevitably lead to unwelcome consequences of one kind or another.

1. **Sit somewhere comfortable where you will not be disturbed. Acknowledge the force of temptation: to remain in a state of denial is to be frozen in time and prevented from moving forward.**
2. **Mentally empty your mind and body of all intention. Think of yourself as a shell temporarily possessed by the fires of temptation.**
3. **In your imagination summon salamander: although it may seem alien to us, it is actually shaped not unlike a miniature human being. It is not too difficult to imagine its body within your body, its limbs within your limbs.**
4. **Imagine the cold dowsing power of salamander taking the heat out of the material self. As your appetites cool, you sense the return of the rational spirit – not reason exactly, but a profound sense of balance and grace.**

LOG LIFE

The idea that the salamander lived in fire undoubtedly derived from an erroneous deduction. In fact, these little creatures lived in the cracks in logs. When the logs were burned on a fire, naturally enough the salamanders shot out. This story points to the importance of not jumping to conclusions. Do not assume that all strong feelings must be resisted. Your shamanic intuition will tell you when the destiny that is tugging at your heart is true and noble.

BUTTERFLY

METAMORPHOSIS

Russian folktale tells of a paper kite that says to a butterfly, "I am lofty and I soar higher above than you. Confess that you are envious." "No," answers the butterfly, "You are always tied and I fly where I choose, while you are the tool of another's foolish amusement."

The butterfly is always in the process of metamorphosis, busy recreating itself. It begins life as a tiny egg, then it becomes a hungry, wandering, leaf-eating caterpillar; in its next stage it is encased in a chrysalis and finally comes its emergence as a fabulous butterfly.

The flitting butterfly jumps and darts about and, try as you might, it is very difficult to catch. Butterflies are some of the earth's most gorgeous creatures. But what is a butterfly? It is a worm that has transformed into a beautiful, colorful being. Let the butterfly spirit lift you on its lovely wings to a metamorphosis of your own.

As humans have evolved, butterfly has become their great ally. Transitions are an inevitable part of a lifetime, and butterfly is there to help you with the changes you are going through. When you wish to reform your life, look to butterfly for the power of metamorphosis. Ask the butterfly spirit to speed up the change to your circumstances. If you are locked in a static situation, call on butterfly for spirited courage to move on.

If butterfly is your spirit animal, you are a charming and happy person, finding beauty wherever you go. You are mercurial and can use your quick wit to easily shift conditions -- you can always lift the mood of an occasion. Use your butterfly power to give life to the places you inhabit or encounter, and to help yourself and other people to transform themselves by shaking off old habits or perhaps even ascending to a new level of being. Lift people up from despair on wings of hope and trust, but always be careful not to engage in rash, frivolous behavior.

THE FLYING FLOWER DANCE

The Native American people known as Hopi, meaning the "people of peace", come from the high, dry plateaux of northeastern Arizona. The Hopi live on *mesas*, or flat-topped mountains, in adobe housing complexes known as *pueblos*. The winters are bitingly cold, but the people patiently await the coming of spring, when the butterflies will show their wings. The arrival of these "flying flowers" signals a time of renewal. Butterflies are regarded as life-bringers and perform the important job of pollinating the crops so that there will be seed.

A traditional butterfly dance is held after the harvest. This dance is a celebration and a social event with deep spiritual significance. It is a prayer for balance and the wisdom of green growing things, because butterflies are associated with the rain that makes the corn grow. At the heart of the dance is a recognition of the changing seasons: a pollination of the spirit and the acknowledgment of past and future generations. For the dance Hopi maidens wear colorful dresses and *tablita* – elaborately carved headdresses in the stylized shape of a butterfly.

Devise a butterfly dance of your own, and perform it on a summer's day when butterflies are on the wing.

OWL

THE MIND OF THE AGES

Owls represent inner knowledge combined with ancient wisdom. They are supreme hunters and their eyes are designed to be able to receive the slightest glimmer of light. For them, one candle is enough to light the entire forest. The dimmer the light is, the better: the light of day is overwhelming for owls and they become quite disoriented, blinking painfully at the unwanted brightness. There are many varieties of owls such as the screech owl, great horned owl, barn owl, snowy owl and the burrowing owl – there are 134 species in the owl tribe.

Weather forecasting was an important function in traditional agrarian cultures, and both the owl and the crow had much to do with the practice. Shamans carefully watched the birds' behavior, from which they deduced impending weather conditions. Long ago, so it is told, when humans and animals spoke the same language, one or other of the birds would address the shaman and inform him about forthcoming changes in the weather.

Owl is sometimes called the "night eagle" and is a friend of the moon. If you see or hear owls at night and you think they are trying to tell you something, you are probably right. They are asking you to look deeply into your own nature. With owl as your spirit animal, you will be a night person and cherish the small hours. Owl people are walking lie detectors, and even when people try to deceive them, deep down they know the truth. They have psychic and clairvoyant powers. With owl as your ally, you will have great intuition in seeing the ulterior motives of others. You could easily be a magician, metaphysician, occultist, cabbalist, shaman or seer. You may be pulled toward the dark powers, but only to understand them, of course – that is, you will never use black magic or the dark arts to interfere with the path of another or to profit from your inexplicable owl powers.

OWL ENERGY

Connect with wisdom Athena was the Greek goddess of wisdom and the owl was her messenger. The bird was protected and large numbers nested in her temple. Be friendly toward owls as Athena was.

Wear an owl amulet In ancient Babylon owls were believed to protect pregnant women, and amulets depicting the bird have been found in many ancient sites. Fashion your own amulet and use it to protect your sleep.

Walk the forest at night Although we lack the visual acuity of owls, we can improve our night vision by walking in the countryside at night. Choose a moonlit night for your first outing and select a broad, open path where you won't lose your bearings. Listen for the sounds of the night and try to interpret them.

OWLS IN FOLKTALES

Owls are important in many European folktales. In Poland it was believed that married women turned into owls when they died. The birds were much admired for their beauty and it was thought that they emerged at night only because other birds, jealous of them, would attack during the day. In the Lorraine area of France owls were called upon to help unmarried women find a partner and in Romania the snowy owl was held to be the soul of repentant sinners flying to heaven.

SALMON

BACK TO THE SOURCE

In Celtic mythology, the salmon is associated with wisdom and the eternal return. It is wise to go to the source of life for answers, and going back to the source is the salmon's journey. The newly hatched young salmon travels far out in the ocean, only to find its way back hundreds or even thousands of miles to the river of its origin – no one knows how. Then, against impossible odds, the intrepid fish pinpoints the precise location where it was hatched, lays its own eggs and the journey begins anew with the next generation of salmon repeating the process.

Salmon show great perseverance in returning to the place of their beginnings, swimming upriver until they either arrive safely or perish. They battle with every sort of enemy, and it is amazing that so many survive. They are a marvelous sight to behold, displaying their glittering hues as they leap against the current into the air to negotiate waterfalls and other hazards. If successful in reaching their destination, they create a sort of trench in the gravely river bottom and there deposit their spawn. Once the young "fry" are hatched, they strike out for the sea.

The salmon tribe can be found throughout the world, inhabiting the coast of the North Atlantic and Pacific Oceans. Wherever there are salmon they are revered by the native populations. Salmon figure prominently as totem pole figures and in celebrations, songs and dances.

If salmon is your spirit animal, you can return to the inner source and offer valuable help to others. You carry the past and have determination, never hesitating to swim against the current. You are brave and will face any obstacle to get to where you want to go. You are impulsive and sometimes have only your instincts to guide you. Perhaps you have foreknowledge of future events. Your special ability is to help lost souls find their way home.

In ancient legend, salmon were once human, but they preferred their previous time as fish and so they returned to the rivers and the sea. Nevertheless, in shamanic thought humans and salmon remain close relatives. The shamans in northwest Native American cultures possess salmon helping spirits; they know that the salmon is a guardian and friend of the people. While dreaming, the shaman shape-shifts and swims long distances with the salmon.

The "salmon people", as they are called, are speared, smoked and eaten. During the salmon season you can see their orange bodies hanging up and drying in rows on drying racks, a practice that has continued for a thousand years. You, too, can cook a delightful dish of fresh salmon near a campfire on a wooden plank, rubbed with crushed juniper berries and brushed with nut oil. Remember to acknowledge the spirit of the salmon before you feast on it. The backbone of the fish should be given back to the water so that the salmon spirit can find it and return to life.

SEAL

FLUIDITY IN LIFE

According to the Inuit people, the seal abides in the waters of Sedna, the mother of oceans, and is known as Old Food Bucket of the North. Sedna gives her blessings to the seals, which were once her fingers before they were chopped off by her evil father, who was being pursued by her giant seabird husband. She was clinging to his kayak when her fingers were sliced away by the cowardly father's knife and she fell into the sea. As the beautiful young woman sank beneath the waves, she was transformed into the goddess of the icy ocean, Sedna, the sustainer of life. Her fingers became seals and various other forms of sea life – food for the people. A simple prayer to the goddess is, "Sacred Sea Mother, may there always be food upon my table."

To Celtic folk, the sea is enchanted, inhabited by mermaids and other mysterious creatures. These mythic beings are seen from the misty shore with their heads bobbing in the water. According to several Celtic legends, "selkies", the word for seals in the Scottish Orkney Islands dialect, can shed their skins and become human, and later put their skins back on and become seals once more. Selkie tales are usually sad ones of faithless lovers and unrequited love. During their stay on land, the selkie folk long for their sea home and sooner or later return to it. The unfortunate abandoned humans pine away for their lost loves for the rest of their (usually short) lives.

It is an old saying that a drop of water contains the whole ocean. We are taught that we are individuals, but we are not the drop – we are the ocean. Seal knows this, and that all life comes from water. Water has always been used in initiation rites, and it teaches us that our personal reality is forever changing. Seal energy speaks to us of the power of being fluid. If the seal is your totem, perhaps you are being told to be more fluid and to move with the currents of change.

THE WALRUS

Walruses, like seals, belong to the scientific order of pinnipeds. The walrus lives in the Arctic regions. It is huge and clumsy with an odd-shaped, rounded head featuring a bulging muzzle. Its upper lip is covered with thick bristles and it has two long, ivory upper canine teeth rather like the tusks of an elephant. The skin is wrinkled and brownish, and there are flat flippers on the back and front legs. Walruses live in herds that will rush against an enemy to protect young and old animals. In contrast to the gentle seal, the walrus is ferocious. If walrus is your spirit animal, you are a keeper of esoteric knowledge and are attracted to secretive esoteric groups.

Except for its tusks, the walrus looks like the fat man from the circus wearing a too big wetsuit and cumbersome flippers. Yet it has access to the secrets of the sea, the austerity of the cold north and has the toughness needed to withstand hostile forces.

HOW TO CONNECT TO SEAL ENERGY

Swim in wild water *Swimming pools are enclosed environments. To truly connect with the fluid freedom of the seal, try swimming in rivers, lakes and, of course, the ocean.*

Meditate in the bath *Tune into the element of water by practicing meditation in the bath. Light candles around the bath, turn off any electric lights and slowly immerse yourself in the water.*

Practice deep breathing *Seals can hold their breath for nearly two hours under water – an extraordinary feat. Learn from the seal – a mammal that has made the sea its home. We, too, can change and adapt with our environment. Learn to be at home in fluidity.*

PEACOCK

EYES OF COMPASSION

A peacock is not much larger in actual body size than a grown chicken, but its feathering is so immense that its total length can measure over 5ft (1.5m). The peacock is a stunning creature, a bird of true splendor. Like the Argus, the watchful giant in Greek mythology with a hundred eyes, the peacock can lay claim to the title Chief of Eyes, and is accordingly named the Argus Peacock in Sumatra. With its robes of bright plumage in the most unusual tints and hues, this bird can be mesmerizing. It often stands in solitude, its long, beautiful tail becoming a trembling fan of dazzling colors.

The peacock spirit was traditionally called upon by priests to bring rain, and the bird is also reputed to confer much good luck, magnificence, truthfulness and serenity. Peacock feathers are used on Hindu altars of worship; with their many brilliant eyes, these feathers symbolize compassion, which often springs from observation of another's needs.

In particular, the bird is associated with the Hindu deity Murugan, the god of war popular in southern India. Murugan is often depicted riding a peacock, which symbolizes his destruction of the ego. In Buddhism the bird is linked with Avalokiteshvara, the bodhisattva of compassion.

People with peacock as a spirit animal are walking a sacred, spiritual path, and are filled with love for all of life. The peacock's eye represents the Third Eye, the eye that destroys illusion and brings an understanding of universal truth.

The peacock reminds us to open our spiritual eyes and see honestly with a new vision. Then we will be able to see beyond the ordinary limits of the senses. We see, hear and feel the higher vibrations of discernment; false beliefs become unraveled and higher knowledge emerges.

A Third-Eye Meditation

This meditation is for your personal growth, so never criticize yourself for any reason during the exercise.

1. Make sure that you will not be disturbed. Find a quiet, comfortable place to sit and breathe deeply for several breaths. Before you begin this meditation, consider the peacock. It walks along with its train of feathers dragging behind, then suddenly stops and opens a fan of those feathers into a glorious display of eyes. See that image in your mind's eye and project it into your forehead. Say a little prayer for the earth and all its people and animals, and for the alleviation of the suffering of all sentient life. Feel completely calm and at ease.
2. Concentrate on each breath while you inhale deeply and fully. Close your eyes and bring your attention to a place on your forehead between your eyebrows. Imagine that you are breathing from this point. Open your consciousness and focus on your breath. When a tiny white dot of light appears inside your inner vision, you are at the gate. You have opened the shades a crack to see truth, to see beyond illusion.
3. As you exhale, feel the light expand and feel a warmth in your forehead. Let the light increase so that you are not a separate part of anything. You are beginning to come to terms with your real self, the unborn and undying transcendent light – the light that always was and always will be.
4. When you feel that your meditation is complete, slowly open your physical eyes. Try to practice this meditation a few minutes every day.

CRANE

SERENITY IN CHANGE

Cranes are large birds with long legs but without the webbed feet of other birds that spend their time among the reeds and bulrushes of the marshlands. The embodiment of confidence and grace, cranes fly with their long neck extended. Some cranes migrate thousands of miles, while others remain on their home turf.

Cranes are known for their elaborate and frolicsome mating dances. This courtship and bonding dance is an eye-catching male and female animal ballet. The birds emit shattering musical cries, bow to each other, jump, twirl and skip, and then move feather to feather side by side, sometimes performing for several minutes.

The elegant crane stands perfectly still on the water's edge, the feet of one leg submerged, patiently waiting for a fish or frog to swim by. It looks like a statue, standing motionless for hours, watching with intense concentration. The beauty of this graceful bird makes it appear fragile and helpless, but this is far from the case. In fact, the crane is studied in martial arts as a master of outfighting, defending from a distance and not letting an opponent get too close, battling with poise and polish. It displays a smooth action in striking with great accuracy using its beak.

When you see a formation of cranes trumpeting and flying high overhead, you are witnessing a small part of eternity. Crane is the wise bird with grace of spirit and complete self-control. "All things come to he who waits," is an old saying that can be applied to crane: it teaches serenity and the art of waiting. The crane has no delusions, confusions or illusions. The water flows and the crane thereby receives boundless energy and divine force, but it knows that what you take you must give back. Its qualities of self-knowledge and reflective understanding offer us serenity in our changing world.

A Morning Crane Meditation for Serenity

The mind can restore itself through the art of meditation. Crane teaches tranquility and the wisdom of emptiness, and no matter what turmoil is going on around you, you can find peace and serenity. This meditation can be done anywhere in or near nature, but it's best performed outside, standing barefoot in dew-wet grass at sunrise and facing east.

1. **Pray to the crane spirit and ask that it be with you. Imagine the crane spirit growing from within – perfectly still, steady and contained. Let any tension flow out of your body and down through your feet into Mother Earth. Be comfortable and relaxed. Look at the early morning shadows and feel any wind that crosses your body. Salute the sun.**
2. **Close your eyes. With toes pointing slightly inward, rock easily back and forth until you find a place of balance and become perfectly still. You will find that when you achieve stillness and your mind calms.**
3. **Now go forward in your imagination into your day. Visualize yourself in perfect control whatever the circumstances. See yourself relaxed, calm and serene. Promise yourself to take deep breaths during the day. Vow to feed your body, mind and spirit with good food. Like the crane, see yourself overcoming any challenges and meeting any changes with unflustered grace and courage. Become still and in a blissful state for as long as you like.**
4. **Acknowledge the crane and its energy, thanking the crane and bringing your consciousness back into your body. Become centered in the day and salute the sun while remembering the crane spirit.**

TIGER

LYING IN WAIT

Weighing up to 600 lb (270kg) and growing to 11ft (3.5m) long, tigers are the "king of the jungle" in eastern Asia. The tiger can bring down animals far larger than itself, either in the water or on land, and has been known to kill adult rhinoceroses, crocodiles and, of course, humans. This, and the belief that parts of the tiger have magical powers, have made this predator one of the most endangered on earth.

Because of its immense size, the tiger has extraordinary physical power, making it the fiercest big cat in existence. Of course, this is its allure, turning the tiger into the ultimate trophy. For centuries, tiger parts have been coveted for their supposed aphrodisiac qualities, but thankfully trade in such tiger products has now been halted in most nations.

The tiger's coat is a graphic play of dramatic black stripes on a vibrant orange background, which, like the jaguar's spots, provides excellent camouflage in the jungle. It is odd that such a flamboyant display of nature actually provides the tiger with the power of invisibility.

The tiger is ferocious, and a symbol of physical power and fearlessness. This power can be harnessed in your own life by connecting with this animal totem. Imagine a tiger, *your* tiger, walking by your side throughout the day. This animal is your protector and the two of you are linked by an intuitive understanding that transcends words. One low growl from your power tiger alerts you to danger or even to your own tendency to veer from the track of your life's purpose. Use this animal totem in all situations where fearlessness is needed and where you can benefit from being invisible.

A Tiger Meditation

This meditation is best practiced at night when tiger energy is at its most powerful.

1. **Sit somewhere comfortable, where you will not be disturbed. Close your eyes and take several deep breaths. Feel yourself centered and calm. In your mind's eye, take yourself deep into the jungle. Feel the heat and humidity, see the outline of trees and ferns. It's dark but your senses are alive and alert.**
2. **As you walk through the undergrowth, be aware of your movements as powerful yet graceful and quiet. You are extraordinarily fluid in motion.**
3. **You enjoy sensing your muscles working as you pad stealthily by. You are a tiger – proud, fearless, king of the jungle. You are lord of all you survey.**
4. **You choose now to disappear into the night. Seamlessly you fade from view. You elect when and where you go – and now it is time to leave.**
5. **Open your eyes and breathe normally. Give yourself a few moments to bring yourself back to the here and now.**

"TIGER, TIGER BURNING BRIGHT!"

The tiger does indeed "burn bright", as the poet William Blake puts it, in many Eastern cultures. In Hinduism, the creature symbolizes sexual passion and unbridled libido, while the great Hindu god Shiva wears a tiger pelt, symbolizing omnipotence. The goddess Shakti or Durga rides a tiger, representing the infinite creative force of the feminine.

The third animal of the Chinese zodiac, the tiger holds tremendous cultural importance in China. Reflecting the way in which intricate martial arts moves tend to be based on specific animal behavior, "Crouching tiger, hidden dragon" is a Chinese metaphor for instinctively hiding your power and strength from others. As it crouches in the underbrush, its muscles quivering and poised to take its prey, the tiger is a formidable beast. Lie low, hoard your power, strike when the time is right – in everything from starting a creative project to confronting a relative about unreasonable attitudes, the tiger's way makes sense.

HIPPOPOTAMUS

MUD MAGIC

Hippopotamus means "river horse" in ancient Greek. This is the third largest land animal and can weigh up to 3 tons (3,000kg). Naturally bad-tempered, hippopotamuses have been known to attack humans and boats.

Hippopotamuses are ferocious protectors of their young, and mothers are capable of killing bull hippos that threaten their calves. The ancient Egyptians recognized the powerful maternal instincts of the hippopotamus, and their goddess Tawaret, protector of pregnant women, was depicted with a hippopotamus's head. These animals are not buoyant in water, but sink to the river bottom where they push off to propel themselves back to the surface for a breath of air. Hippopotamuses are happiest wallowing in deep, viscous pools of slimy, thick mud; in fact, mud is their milieu, the denseness of dark river mud supporting their enormous weight like a well-worn mattress. This thick mud also coats their hairless skin and protects them from the sun's scorching rays and aggressive stinging insects. In short, the hippopotamus gains its support, power and protection from mud.

Having hippopotamus as an animal totem can help you use confusion to your advantage. Are you in a situation where people predict your reactions? Turn the tables and do the unexpected: laugh when you are expected to cry and be serene in the face of aggression. Hippopotamus energy is grounded and heavy like the earth and yet entirely pliant like water.

Call on the hippopotamus totem to travel between opposites. These unusual creatures are aggressive and violent, yet they are tender and protective of their young. They live in the water yet they cannot swim or float. Their huge bulk supported by squat legs makes them appear slow and dawdling, but they can outrun a man. Hippopotamuses derive their power from dichotomies -- they remain a mystery.

PELOTHERAPY

Hippopotamuses practice pelotherapy, the medical term for therapeutic treatments using mud. It is a class of natural medicine used in ancient healing practices. Making up more than 70 percent of the human body, water cleanses and purifies and has healing properties. Water and earth are both indispensable for life and its processes, one symbolizing fluidity and change, the other providing the necessary grounding and the wherewithal for shelter. Earth is the womb-principle, water is energizing transformation. Mixed together, these two powerful elements yield mud.

Mud contains minerals, and some kinds of mud are able to draw toxicity out of the body, using the skin as a door – according to ayurvedic science, skin is the "mouth of the bone". In this way, mud can address imbalances deep within the body, with various mixtures of mud and clay being used to treat disease. Be inspired by the hippopotamus and try your own form of mud bathing for healing and rejuvenation.

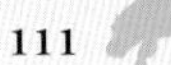

HARE

EARS TO THE SKY

With their tall, wide, funnel-shaped, black-tipped ears, which are slightly longer than their heads, hares have pronounced listening skills and are intimate with the sounds of creation. They are able to analyze sounds with pinpoint accuracy and determine their exact meanings.

Hares are often mistaken for rabbits, but their fur is redder and they have very long "thumper" hind legs and a black tail – although they do have many traits in common with rabbits. The hare knows when to move out of harm's way to safety, being always ready to bolt. This animal thinks and moves fast, and at the merest hint of trouble bounds off and runs madly away.

Hares have ingenuity and use their wit, employing clever maneuvers to elude predators and throw them off the scent. For example, the hare will run in a straight line, hide and then return the way it came, thereby leaving confused signs of its whereabouts. A hare will also make leaps at right angles from the direction in which it is traveling, then go back to its original path, thus diverting the hunter.

Three hares linked together in a circle form a motif found in sacred sites in the Far East, Middle East and Europe. It is believed to be associated with fertility and the lunar cycle. It is interesting that many cultures, including those of India, China, Japan and Mexico, recognize a hare in the dark patches of the moon, suggesting this animal has always been seen as having otherworldly associations.

Hare has sharp perception, hearing any vibrations and picking up on clues, going beyond distortions to the foundation. If the ultra-sensitive hare is your spirit animal, you will hear the call and answer it – the subtle call moving you along your path.

THE HARE IN THE MOON

Anyone drawn to the moon would do well to take hare as their spirit animal – or rabbit if they prefer. Both creatures are proverbially prolific; and both appear and vanish with the stealth of shadows, like the moon itself. The German fertility goddess known as Eostra owned a hare in the moon that laid eggs, symbolizing the renewal of life, around the time of her spring festival – this is the origin of Easter eggs (the name comes from Eostra) and the Easter rabbit.

In Chinese legend a girl named Chang'e was stranded on the moon after she stole a pill that granted immortality. Finding that she could fly, she headed for the moon, pursued by her husband, Houyi, an exiled immortal, who was turned back to earth by strong winds. Once on the lunar surface, she coughed up the pill, and then ordered the hare who lives on the moon to make her another, using his pestle and mortar, so that she could return to her husband. The hare is still up there, pounding away. The husband built himself a palace in the sun (yang), Chang'e a palace in the moon (yin). Every month Houyi visits Chang'e and the moon glows full with particular beauty.

OX

DETERMINATION AND PERSISTENCE

The ox is very important in many agrarian societies. Oxen are stronger than horses and are therefore widely used to draw carts and ploughs. In the Hindu tradition all cattle, including oxen, are venerated and their slaughter is forbidden. The Lord Shiva is said to ride the back of a great bull, Nandi, while Lord Krishna was raised in a family of cowherders.

Oxen eat an enormous amount of grass and other vegetable matter, and spend much of the day chewing the cud, which is in fact a second chewing. The food is swallowed once and then it is regurgitated in the form of a soft, round ball (bolus), which is then re-chewed and re-swallowed. Cud chewing helps the ox digest its food more effectively, so that it ingests more, which in turn gives the animal good health and endurance.

In various Asian countries, these lords of the plough are used to predict agricultural yields for the coming year. Oxen are ritually offered various foods, such as rice, seeds, hay and maize, and even an assortment of drinks. What the oxen choose to eat and drink is telling, and the shaman or oracle makes a forecast according to what selections the animals make. Whether feast or famine, these predictions are usually accurate.

If you are in a situation where you need determination and perseverance (in short, persistence) call on ox power. Untiring, loving and giving, oxen never fail to perform their duties. With ox as a spirit totem, you will always strive to be of service and go the distance. No one can mistake your great strength, inner calm and peacefulness. You are most resolute, ploughing all the way to the end and making the fields bear fruit. Call on the spirit of ox for maturity and indomitable willpower, and then plough the good furrows of your life. Where you have toiled, there will be plenty.

TUNE INTO OX ENERGY

Practice cow face pose This seated yoga pose involves crossing the legs over each other while bending the left arm up behind the back and lifting the right arm down over the shoulder, the aim being to link the hands behind your back. The crossed legs are said to resemble the lips of a cow.

Make imagery The ancestor of the ox, the aurochs, was depicted in prehistoric cave paintings including those at Lascaux. Honor your ox spirit by drawing or painting your own powerful beast.

Cast your runes The aurochs gave its name to the letter U in the runic alphabet, which was used in Northern Europe prior to the adoption of the Latin alphabet. Meditate on the aurochs rune as a way of understanding the importance of this animal's energy to our ancestors.

Dance with Krishna In his childhood and youth the god Krishna lived with cowherders and earned the names "Govinda", which means "finder of cows", and "Gopala", which means "protector of cows". You can gain wisdom by meditating on Krishna's sympathy with your power animal.

ON THE TRAIL OF THE OX

In the 12th century a Chinese Zen master painted ten pictures depicting the search for an ox – an allegory for the search for satori, *the realization of our true nature. The seeker catches the ox, tames it and rides it home – but then forgets about it. The picture after this is a blank, the next shows the simple life, then finally the seeker returns to the market in a mood of happy generosity. At last the herder is at peace with all sentient life, enjoying interaction with his companions.*

OCTOPUS

COPING SKILLS

In the past, the octopus was frequently envisaged as a giant sea monster. Many works of art illustrate a master schooner under full sail crushed in the coiling, writhing tentacles of a huge octopus, with sailors leaping into the boiling sea. But there are other more positive concepts relating to the octopus. It was a symbol of the center of the flux of creation. The creature has eight appendages, just as the Hindu goddess Dhanya Lakshmi has eight arms, and eight is a spiritual number, signifying balance, equilibrium and justice, fulfilment and completion.

The octopus has a large, convex, spoon-shaped head set with big complex eyes, and from this head its eight limbs extend. With those legs it propels itself along the sandy sea-floor, and each leg has two rows of suckers. Octopuses have large brains and are highly intelligent and adaptable. They also deliver poisonous bites. In fact, the egg-sized Australian blue-ringed octopus can kill a human with its bite – without immediate medical attention, breathing will stop and the heart will fail. The octopus can change color and blend into any environment, and when it becomes seriously threatened, it can disappear in a great cloud of ink.

The person who befriends octopus is swift to grasp the meaning of things. This creature reduces stress by coping and does not bother trying to change the unchangeable. It moves by a forceful propulsion and solves problems where it can – quickly and efficiently. People with octopus as their spirit animal stay away from the limelight. When the boss realizes how you are multi-tasking and getting eight things done at once, he or she may want to acknowledge your achievements and reward you – but the spotlight is not for you. With the spirit power of octopus, you will gain momentous skills at coping with difficult situations.

BECOMING OCTOPUS

Vase painting The Minoan people celebrated all forms of sea life. A famous vase dated *c.*1500BC depicts an octopus splayed over the round surface of the vase. Celebrate your octopus spirit with art – paint your own octopus bowl or vase, with tentacles looping around it.

Meditate on Dhanya Lakshmi This eight-armed goddess of the harvest is one of a group of eight goddesses associated with prosperity, knowledge, strength and power. Create an altar to this deity and place upon it the objects associated with her – the lotus, sugar cane and bananas – to thank her for her generosity.

Snorkel Coral reefs are one of the favored habitats of the octopus. Go snorkeling. Immerse yourself in your spirit animal's world.

KWAKIUTL OCTOPUS MASK

The Canadian Kwakiutl people live on the west coast of British Colombia. Their culture is based on the potlatch festival in which wealth is redistributed. They produce fine totem poles and their ceremonial dances are alive with magic and spirit power. Kwakiutl shamans receive powers from a dream spirit and often carve superb masks, including the octopus mask, to honor them in ceremonial dances. These powers are usually kept highly secret. The Kwakiutl call the octopus the "bear of the rocks".

In one of their legends, a fishing expedition failed to return. Clam Shell Boy wanted to know why, so he paddled out to an island. On a rock shelf, he found scattered bones and the den of a man-eating octopus. Clam Shell Boy asked a shaman what to do about it. "Kill the monster by piercing it four times with a sharpened stick rubbed with octopus blood," the shaman instructed. This Clam Shell Boy did. When the octopus died, the spirit of a man came out of him and said, "You have killed me, so now you will have my powers and the right to wear my face." This is how the sacred octopus mask came into being.

CHAPTER 4

Inner Beauty

Certain animals have an obvious connotation of elegance – for example, the dove and the gazelle, which begin this chapter. The honeybee's hive is a pleasingly harmonious image of human co-operation, while honey is a metaphor of spiritual sustenance. Whale song, a swan's majestic flight, the elusiveness of the snow leopard, the brilliance of the hummingbird, the playfulness of the dolphin – all these take their place alongside dove and gazelle without incongruity. Other creatures make up in character and symbolism for what they lack in grace. The fox has been introduced for his virtuoso acrobatics of thought; the cow for her unspectacular purity and kindness; the panda as a graphic embodiment of yin and yang. By helping us to develop our potential, all animals – even the wily, stolid or apparently comical – can contribute to our inner beauty.

DOVE

SECRETS OF ASTRAL FLIGHT

In the story of the Great Flood in the Old Testament, Noah, confined to his ark full of animals, sent out a dove to find out if there was any habitable land. After several attempts, a dove returned with an olive leaf, and Noah knew that the flood was subsiding.

Astral travelers often use the dove for similar missions, in their quest to seek out useful information. Shamans have different belief systems concerning the nature of the outward world. According to Huichol myth, Mother Dove Girl became the mother of the boy who became the sun. The bird carries the great light, and the dove is repeatedly depicted surrounded by the glorious rays of the sun. For the shaman, the dove became an opening through which he or she could bi-locate. The process or phenomenon by which this transpires is known as astral flight. In Christian iconography, the dove is seen in spirit form as the Holy Ghost.

Accordingly, we have two bodies, a host body and a spirit body. With practice, the spirit body (dove) can leave the host through the heart chakra and journey out of our physical being. The key to this art is to present to the spirit body a set of coordinates or even a mental map – a clear path to where you want your spirit body to go is imperative. Purity of heart and pure intentions are the rule. Shamans in their spirit travels may go to the bottom of the deepest sea and fly to the moon. They may spy on an enemy village or consult with the sister winds to see how the weather is going to change.

Dove will give you the ability to know intuitively what is happening at a distance. The dove spirit brings you the power of lucid dreaming, or dreaming in a state of wakefulness, in order to see events happening in the "real world". Many people with dove as their spirit animal have the ability to shape-shift and travel the astral planes.

A Dove Astral Exercise

Spirit animals can facilitate astral travel, which is simply the act of intentionally extending your spiritual eyes. Astral traveling means training the soul to assume an astral body, so that you can locate and investigate another place in spirit form. Shamans were master astral travelers in tribal societies, but we can all learn the skills. The following exercise is an aid to your own astral flight.

1. **Make yourself comfortable and relaxed in a darkened room. Select a location or person you want to visit and then hold that thought in your mind.**
2. **Close your eyes and breathe energy into your heart chakra (see page 47). When the energy is strong, visualize it as a ball of searing white light. Out of this light let a beautiful white dove emerge, fly from your body and hover just above you. Stay in the dove form and go to your desired destination.**
3. **Do not be afraid of what you see, hear or experience. Explore for a while. When you are satisfied, tell the dove to take you back to your body. Let the astral dove energy dissolve into the ball of light in your heart chakra. Breathe deeply and completely relax. Thank the light. Thank the dove for helping you and promise to visit again.**

A DOVE TALISMAN

With its beauty, the dove is associated with the feminine. Wear a dove talisman for peace and tranquility. A dove charm is traditionally touted as a protection against the evil eye and other types of psychic attack. The dove is used as a symbol of purity and sublime spirituality, and it can also represent the vow of love for another. It symbolizes a spiritual rebirth, and is often encountered in Christian iconography, where the soul lifts from a saint's body after death. Some Native American cultures also believed that the dove symbolized a cycle of life, death and rebirth.

GAZELLE
SILENT SONG

A panic on the veldt – the wafting scent of a lion! The gazelle lifts her head from a tuft of grass, ears wiggling, intense. Then she bolts . . . bounding, loping in a rhythm with no thought, no effort – she finds the silence and her silent song. She cuts north, feeling the way in front of her – soaring over the blurred ground as if she is the ground itself. With the lion following, the gazelle keeps going, never daring to pause or look back. Her movements are clean and elegant.

Gazelle's name is derived from an older name, "powerful blazing god". The creature is related to the antelope, the peculiar-looking wildebeest and the impala. Gazelle are among the fastest and most graceful animals on earth. Preferring wide savannas, gazelle spend most of their time munching on bush and grass. Both males and females display long-ringed, backward-curved hollow horns ending in a little hook. There are some fourteen species of gazelle ranging throughout Africa and Southwest Asia.

If gazelle is your totem animal, you are fleet and agile of foot. You are able to listen to the changing sounds the wind makes gusting through the grasses. You are aware of the slightest unusual scent. Gazelle power gives you the sure ability to detect threats to your well-being. You will respond instantly with unpredictable action and bounding speed. You can confuse a situation with zigzagging shifts of direction that leave others mystified.

With your gazelle totem's guidance you will always triumph over baseness and vulgarity. The creature has great awareness and gives the power to communicate silently with others on deeper levels. Your presence and vulnerability are important strengths. Your life song is a healing song. A close relationship with your gazelle totem will sharpen your instincts and improve your listening skills. You will become more focused and be able to live in the moment.

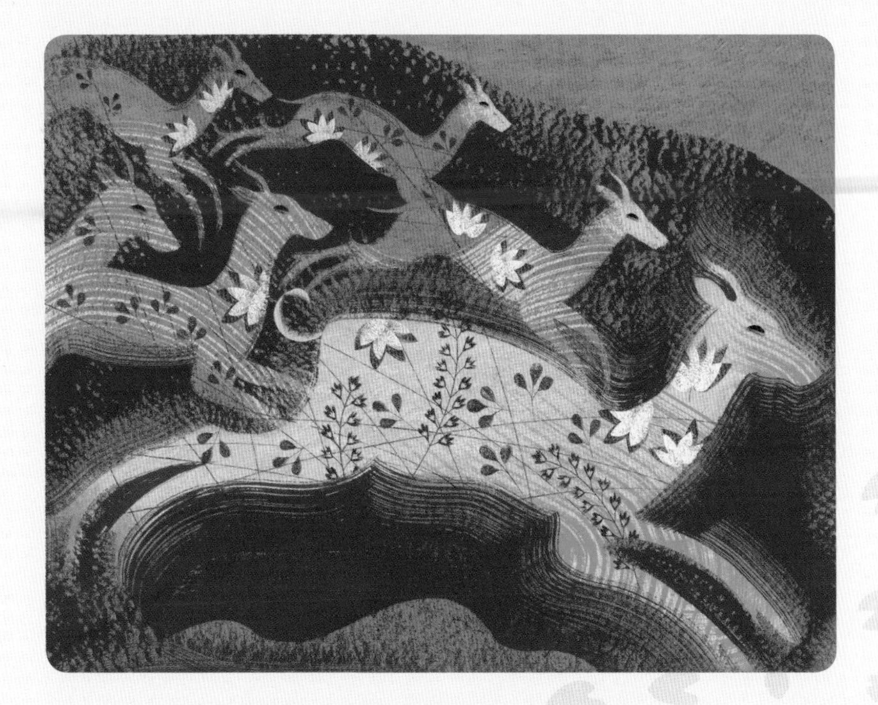

THE GAZELLE IN SUFI POETRY

Gazelle's horns curve back like a lyre, the instrument of poets. The animal was associated with the Great Prophet and with splendor itself – and with the elusive beauty of God. In ancient Sufi poetry and song, the gazelle was a symbol of the moon god. Rumi, the twelfth-century Sufi mystic and one of the world's greatest poets, believed that poets are simply interpreters of the word of God. He and other Sufi poets wrote in the *ghazal* (gazelle) form, of rhyming couplets and a refrain. The *ghazal* form is noted for the purity of its spiritual content.

Several Sufi poets compared the soul to flowing water and the material world to ice. Our souls are trapped in ice which will melt in the fires of life and our soul force will be freed once more. In another instructive Sufi poem, the soul is in a closed coffin that one day is opened. If we can't find realization in this world, how can we hope to find it in the next? The whirling, spiraling dervish dance was said to be inspired by Rumi – a dance that leads inward to the perfect stillness of the silent breath of eternity.

HONEYBEE

THE BEAUTY OF WORK

The honeybee has always been a symbol for love's labor. The bee teaches the beauty and fulfilment of work – work being a true spiritual and material joining. Bees are used as a symbol of the soul and the soul's mission – of gathering, quickening, revitalization, returning to sweetness and exuberance. Bees teach us to recover our enthusiasm. Bring your passion, your bliss into your work and your work will be satisfying. Bees represent sweetness and light because of their sweet honey and the beeswax that is used for candle-making.

Few creatures are as important to human life as bees. It has been calculated that every third bite of food we take can be traced to the work of the bees pollinating plants. Bees buzz patiently over field and flower. The hive community is active and vital, making the comb and generating honey. The bee licks the sweet secretion (nectar) from flowers, swallows it and stores it in its internal honey sac. At the hive the honey is deposited in a six-sided wax cell. The cell structure is a mathematical marvel, providing the greatest strength and space with the least amount of material.

There are cave paintings showing beekeeping, an art that goes back to the Stone Age. In ancient Egypt bees were a sun symbol. Bees were born from the tears of the solar creator god, Ra. Edible honeycomb has been found in the tombs of Egyptian royalty. Cleopatra, a queen renowned for her great beauty, bathed in milk and honey daily.

With honeybee as your spirit ally, you will discover hidden wisdom – a sweet realization of who you are and what labor you can contribute within your community. On a personal level, with honeybee's help you can accomplish much. Listen to this spirit creature and become more efficient and productive. However, beware of becoming a workaholic. Remember to take breaks and savor the honey.

BECOME A BEEKEEPER

Bees secure our food supply. But worker bees are abandoning hives and simply disappearing. Owing to collapsing hive populations and species endangerment, there has been a growth in backyard beekeeping. Where there are parks, trees, flowers – the basic flora – there is food for bees. Even if you live in an apartment, you can keep bees in various unusual ways, such as on rooftops and balconies. Helping the busy little bees certainly has its benefits – honey, royal jelly, bee pollen, the pollination of your garden plants and superior wax, to name just a few. Scientific research even suggests that beekeepers live longer!

Prepare by learning about beekeeping. There are many good books on the subject. (Obviously, you won't want to keep bees if you are allergic to their stings.) Beekeeping does not take a lot of time or effort, nor does it cost a lot of money. Think about starting your own bee sanctuary. You will need to invest in some bee tools and protective clothing. You will also need a hive, which you can buy or build yourself. As for the bees themselves, there are many sources – you can buy a complete swarm or a starter colony, with or without a hive.

It may take a little gumption to set it all up, but once you do so, you will find that the bees do most of the work. And you will have done your part in preventing the decline and extinction of the honeybee.

ROYAL JELLY

Royal jelly is a milky substance that turns an ordinary bee larva into a queen. It is produced by the hypopharyngeal glands of nursing bees and used to feed the queen bee. On a continued diet of royal jelly the queen grows one and a half times larger than a normal bee, over about three or four years. Royal jelly is a super-food that greatly enhances human health and can be an aid to fertility. It is highly prized and commands a hefty price in the marketplace.

WHALE

POWER SONGS

Whales are mammals, which means that they produce milk and suckle their young. They belong to the same family as dolphins and porpoises, the Cetacea, but this order is generally divided into two suborders, the toothed whales and the baleen whales. Toothed whales include dolphins, as well as the sperm, killer, pilot, orca and beluga whales, while the baleen whales are filter feeders eating small organisms caught in a comb-like structure in their mouth called a baleen. Members of this suborder include the blue, minke and humpback whale.

Humpback whales are famous for their "song" – a series of repeating sounds that can vary both in pitch and loudness. The songs can travel thousands of miles and are unique to the whales occupying that geographical area; whales from different areas sing entirely different songs. Whale songs are considered one of the most complex forms of communication in the animal kingdom and there is much debate about their meaning and purpose. Male humpbacks perform the songs during the mating season so courtship clearly plays an important role. One thing we can say is that the whale song is a power song for that creature and, paradoxically, a power song does not have to have purpose – it can be solely an expression of oneness with nature.

With whale as your spirit animal, you will be given many power songs. You are a magnetic person with a high frequency emanating from a cellular level, and you will have formidable skills of communication. With your great sensitivity to sound and rhythm, poetry and storytelling come easily to you. You will probably be involved in protecting the earth from dark forces – good luck! Your whale spirit animal keeps you high-minded and purposeful. With whale as your totem animal, you will see the big spiritual picture and always seek to make the world a better place to inhabit.

A Whale Circle Meditation

This exercise will attune you to the sensitivity and grace of the whale, its thrilling, floating presence in a cosmos of the unconscious.

1. Lie down and make yourself comfortable. Close your eyes.
2. Begin by meditating on the planet Venus rising in the velvet night. See it as a blue dot. When you can see the blue dot clearly, expand it in your mind to the size of a door you can pass through. Hold the color and enter the blue circle. Pass through to a blue field, breathing in the color blue. Imagine yourself in the ocean depth, partaking of blue whale energy. Feel the whale spirit taking you over. Let your mind loose from its moorings and join with the whale's mind. Feel weightless and wise, an imposing presence in the blue vistas of the ocean.
3. Stay here as long as you like, but when you are ready, return through the blue circle. Let the circle collapse into the blue dot. Let the blue dot become the rising Venus. Say goodbye and thank you to this planet and to all you have experienced. Come back into the actual world, refreshed by your oceanic adventure.

FOX

OUT-OF-THE-BOX THINKING

The fox is crafty, stealthy – a trickster figure. He has a singular cunning. His face is pointed and he has triangular ears. Foxes were once thought to be related to cats, but in fact they are members of the dog (canid) family. Their eye-pupils are almond-shaped, and the amber-eyed fox is quick and sure of foot. They have acute hearing, the ears moving rather like a cupped hand to improve audibility. Foxes also have an extremely developed sense of smell. Unlike dogs and wolves, they are loners – meticulous and solitary hunters. They do not snarl or bark, but are quiet and expressionless. If a fox were trapped inside the innermost of a set of Chinese boxes stacked one inside the other, it would be no problem: he would think himself out of there in a most ingenious manner.

Thinking outside the box means to think differently than others, more creatively and with innovation, and to seek far afield for novel answers or to find simple solutions that are staring you in the face. The fox is unorthodox and has uncanny ingenuity. He understands the hounds and performs the most shrewd maneuvers to throw them off the scent.

Fox tales are found throughout the world in many cultures. In fable, the fox is often a bad character, stealing chickens or hoodwinking a nice but gullible victim. There are fox shamans in Native America and in China the Taoist masters are said to have supernatural powers related to fox – which is to say, the power to create illusions, shape-shifting, and even disappearing and reappearing at will. There are said to be fox wizards in Japan who compound an elixir that prolongs life indefinitely.

With fox as a spirit animal you will solve problems in unusual but wholly workable ways. The fox spirit will tell you to watch what people do, not attend to what they say. With fox as your power animal you will have the ability to read a situation in an instant. Fox confounds and vexes you, thanks to his instant realizations, arriving at an answer before others have even asked the question. Fox covers his tracks, evading those who try to stalk him. Possessed of a super-subtle intelligence, he sees many paths where others see only one, and he uses this multiplicity to his advantage. He understands every nuance of every nuance. By an instant calculation of the possibilities, fox will always arrive at the right course of action in any situation. Those who associate the crafty intelligence of foxes with low morals are missing a point: by putting craft at the service of virtue we can do wonders on virtue's behalf.

DOGON FOX DIVINER

The cliff-dwelling Dogon people live in Mali in West Africa and come from the stars, or so they will tell you. In particular, they are linked with the brilliant star Sirius. The Dogon will also speak of other, invisible stars in the Sirius binary star system. These stars have been recently validated by modern astronomy – exactly as their ancient oral history has described them. Certain icons of the Dogon people depict ancestral lizard-like beings with wings. Their shamans are in contact with these lightyears-distant life forms and receive guidance from them. They claim to have always known the earth's rotation and its elliptical orbit around the sun. They say that there is intelligent life throughout the universe and they teach that animals know our destiny, especially the pale fox.

In his divining, the fox shaman draws a long rectangular rendering in the sand using his finger and sticks, praying for answers all the while. The sacred sand picture is an oracular field, a complex artwork of esoteric inter-dimensional grids depicting human life within the cosmos. The work completed, the shaman calls to the pale fox for answers as he scatters peanuts over his creation.

The shaman leaves and returns in the morning and reads the meaning of the tail marks and footprints left by the pale fox upon the sand grids. When the fox treads upon the grids, his movements are said to shape the future – so it is told by the Dogon fox shaman. The shaman merely interprets the message left by the fox. These messages revealing the future are always accurate.

SWAN

SUBLIME KNOWLEDGE

Seeing the swan on a misty lake on a cold morning is magical. Beautiful and almost diaphanous, the swan can appear like a dream. It glides along regally, trailing ripples on tranquil waters – an exquisite sight. The largest member of the family that includes geese and ducks, this aquatic bird moves gracefully on water, but waddles around like a duck on land. There are seven species of swan, the mute swan being the classic all-white variety with a long neck and an orange-pink bill; in fact, the swan has the longest neck of any bird.

The male swan is called a cob, the female a pen and a baby swan a cygnet. The constellation Cygnus (the Latin word for swan), also called the Northern Cross, is the depiction of a swan with swept-back wings sailing down the river of stars known as the Milky Way. This is one of the more poignant myths of the night skies. The stars tell the story of Queen Leda who was ravished by Zeus in the form of a swan. The union produced Pollux, their son, who with his half-brother Castor later became the twins in the constellation Gemini.

The swan is usually a solar symbol. In some Native American cultures, the swan is the soul and represents the shaman voyaging. Personal totems were classified as dream animals. To dream of a swan was to glimpse the highest heaven and be acknowledged by the celestial spirits. To dream four times of a swan is to become a shaman – a mysterious being with an exquisite spirit. A female shaman is called a "swan" in some northern Native American cultures.

With swan as your spirit animal, you will project a mystical inner beauty. Your direction is north and your season is winter. Swan gives you the ability to know instinctively what to do on all occasions. Social graces come naturally to the swan. You will often have glimpses into the future.

SARASWATI: THE CREATIVE SOURCE

Saraswati is the divine swan maiden, goddess of music, the arts and knowledge. To those who chant the swan goddess's mantra and honor her with meditation and offerings of flowers, fruit and milk sweets, divine knowledge will be revealed.

The Sanskrit word *sara* is "flow" in English, and Saraswati's name means "the flowing waters of life". There is an extinct river that bears her name, and this once fed into the Ganges, the most sacred river in all of India. Seated atop her swan, Saraswati strokes the strings of a lute (symbolizing music, song and poetry) and holds a rosary (prayer and spiritual devotion) and a book (knowledge). Young and fair, with four arms and dressed in white, this goddess bestows spiritual purity, independence, self-transformation, the freedom of inquiry and, of course, creativity and creative flow.

Summon the swan goddess when you need to get your creative energies moving. Fly into the flow.

DEER

MESSENGER OF THE SPIRIT

Deer are ungulates, meaning that they have hooves, and in their case cloven hooves, like pigs and sheep – split into two toes. The deer's eyes are set to the side of its head, giving the animal an extensive, 300-degree view. These animals have superb night vision, although they are color-blind and see only in yellow and blue. They have sharp hearing and can tune into much higher frequencies than humans. Standing perfectly still, the deer's ears will rotate in the direction of the faintest sound.

Shamans of old had deer spirit messengers as helpers and to provide explanations and other clear communication from the supernatural world. The deer spirit is not hindered by distance or time, and deer shamans have the ability to hear and pass messages from other dimensions. They catch the voices of disincarnate beings, perhaps a loved one or a lost relative – even spirits of the unborn. Individuals with deer as their spirit animal have precognitive skills and can predict uncannily and with great accuracy future events down to the slightest detail.

If deer is your personal spirit animal, you will have a calm, kind and quiet nature. Deer has a pacifist personality, easy-going and quick to flee any disturbing situation or threat. You are sensitive to the needs of others. Always pay attention to your deer spirit totem. Deer are unique in that they have antlers, which by and large are found only on male deer – and antler tissue is the fastest-growing animal tissue known. The deer shed their antlers each year and regenerate new ones. In some Native American teachings, deer and other antlers are regarded as antennae that pick up inter-dimensional intelligences and communications from higher life forms. It is said that deer bring messages from supernatural sources and are the messengers of spirit.

The Deer Mudra

The Deer Mudra is a means of using your fingers to assist pranayama breathing, or yogic breath control. Use it as a prelude to meditation. The fisted hand and extended fingers make a shape that resembles a deer's head and antlers. Relish the deep, cleansing breaths of pranayama. Traditionally this exercise uses the right hand, but the left hand can be used instead if you find that easier.

1. **Close your right hand into a fist. Press your index and middle fingers into your thumb base, holding them there firmly.**
2. **Stretch out your ring and little fingers. Press the pad of your ring finger to anchor it behind the little finger's nail. "Fuse" the fingertips to make one.**
3. **Bring your hand to your nose, keeping your head straight, and looking forward. Keep your shoulders level. Tuck your right elbow lightly into your side.**
4. **Close your right nostril with the very tip of your thumb and inhale slowly through your left. Then close your left nostril with the tip of your ring finger and pinky combination and exhale through the right.**
5. **Repeat two or three times, then release the mudra.**

DEER DANCES

The deer is a constant force in nature and a vital spirit power, honored in ritual and ceremony. From Alaska and Canada all the way down to lower Latin America, deer dances are performed. Black-tailed deer dances, fawn dances, little deer dances and many other dances related to deer are still practiced by indigenous tribes in a wide range of styles. Dancers wear costumes portraying the deer, some wearing deer heads and antlers. Deer and antelope dancers use two canes to simulate the walk of these four-legged creatures. Connect with the deer – and dance.

GIANT PANDA

CREATIVE LEISURE

When pandas first came to the West from China, they created a sensation. An elusive creature, the giant panda has a distinctive black and white coloring. It is sad to reflect that this bear, with its great character and charisma, is on the endangered species list. There are estimated to be only about 1,500–2,000 pandas in existence in the wild, and about 150 or fewer in zoos worldwide.

The panda's habitat once covered a vast area of eastern and southern China, as well as Myanmar and North Vietnam. Today the panda lives in various small patches of bamboo forests, and even those are shrinking. Pandas live at elevations of 5,000–10,000ft (1,500–3000m). The forests may be snow-covered or rainy and shrouded in clouds. Unlike that of other bears, the panda's diet is mostly vegetarian. Pandas like their food and spend a great deal of time eating. They can consume over 80 lb (35kg) of bamboo a day – 99 percent of their diet consists of bamboo. From an upright, sitting position, they grasp stalks and other sections of bamboo and devour it.

Pandas are curious and take great pleasure in exploring and discovering their bamboo forest environment. A panda will smell, taste, examine and test everything. Pandas climb trees, skip atop logs and dance through shadows and light. In fact, they are highly acrobatic creatures and engage in all sorts of quirky feats, tumbling on the ground and then springing up.

Although busy animals, pandas also enjoy fun-filled leisure time. If panda is your spirit animal, you have an inner knowledge and a sense of humor. You are able to guide people in times of crisis. Pandas have a certain sensitivity and complete honesty. People with the panda totem are always refreshing and adaptable, as well as intelligent, playful and creative. If you have some leisure time, become inventive and adventurous like the happy, endearing panda. If you have no leisure time, create some.

THE TAO OF PANDA

Pandas are black and white, and Chinese, so what better inhabitant of the animal kingdom to represent the Tao, the sum of yin and yang, of all complementary opposites? Think of this creature as encompassing male and female, and embracing all races. In the balance of energies, nothing is left out: every outsider takes his or her special place in the dance of being. As this is a creature especially popular with children, panda soft toys are fairly easy to come by. If you wish, buy one as the physical manifestation of panda energy. Bear in mind, too, that pandas were often given away by Chinese rulers or dignitaries as diplomatic gifts. With a panda toy, you could imitate this practice – or else let the panda release from your spirit a deep generosity that prompts you to give away something more precious.

BAMBOO

The main food of the giant panda, bamboo has a symbolism that is fascinating in itself. Oriental symbol of resilience, longevity, happiness and spiritual truth, the bamboo is also traditionally linked with the steps to enlightenment on account of its ringed stem. The bamboo's flexibility also conjures up a natural, Taoist form of strength.

COW

PASTORAL PARADISE

"One can measure the greatness of a nation and its moral progress by the way it treats its animals," said Mahatma Gandhi. In India cows are considered holy and shown the utmost respect. There are cow festivals and a single cow is seen as a representative of all other animals. Cows are symbols of abundance and charitable giving, and at least in theory they dwell at all times in a pastoral paradise. Cows also have nearly panoramic vision and can smell what's coming many miles away.

The cow is a lunar and astral symbol, its crescent horns representing the moon; its abundant milk, the countless stars of the Milky Way. Nut, the Egyptian sky goddess, at times reflects this symbolism, for she appears as a cow with stars on her belly, her legs the four quarters of the earth.

Cow is a yin animal, the embodiment of the female principle. She is associated with the moon – the reflective qualities of receptivity, balance and intuition. Cow is the ever-charitable, undemanding provider. She teaches the milk of human kindness and the deep mysteries of mindful lives – a transcendental universal purity.

In Scandinavia there are old stories of the nourisher, the ice cow that emerged from the ice. She licked a lump of ice into the shape of a man, breathed on it and brought forth the first human. When she did this, she started off the adventure we humans call life.

When you hear cowbells, does it send a pang of longing to your heart? That is a hint that cow is your spirit animal. And if cow walks by your side in spirit, consider yourself many times blessed. She imparts feminine generosity and a potential for a hefty new abundance. Cow spirit animal instructs you to love and nurture yourself and to find your ideal home. She is the great mother aspect of your being – strong, giving and calm. The cow mother symbolizes fertility, growth and grounded power.

A Sacred Cow Affirmation

Try these or similar positive affirmations in the early morning.

1. **I call upon the cow spirit to come to me and be with me. I drink your spiritual milk of nourishment and rejuvenation.**
2. **My soul walks in lush green pastures – in waving oceans of soft green grass. I smell the perfume of beautiful, colorful wild flowers. I feel the warmth of the sun and I breathe easily and gently.**
3. **I radiate peace to all of life. Love and kindness surround me.**
4. **I am joyful, and joyfulness is my true nature. Peaceful, loving thoughts light up my life.**
5. **I am happy in the silence, in the stillness. I open myself to receive divine love and guidance. I open myself to bliss.**
6. **I am a radiant being with positive loving energy. I send out unconditional non-judgmental love and the universe reflects it back to me. I radiate good energy and love.**
7. **No matter what noise or confusion occurs, I am always at peace. I walk in truth, beauty, balance and harmony. Love and peace shape my life and my environment.**

SERENITY AMID FAITH

Verses in the Rig-Veda liken the cow to the goddess associated with the mother of the gods. To kill a cow was equated with the wanton murder of a holy being. Cows are the soul of inner stillness and bring serenity even in the midst of chaos. If you simply spend time with or near one, the purity of the cow can lift base level energy to a higher vibration. In India cows are seen wandering the streets and eating garbage which is transformed into purity and sacred fire when the cow dung is burned. Steady toil, patience and great strength are their immediate gifts. The cow totem gives inner peace.

THUNDERBIRD

THE VOYAGING SOUL

It is a misconception that Native Americans believed literally in an enormous bird with eyes that shot lightning and flapping wings that made thunder. The thunderbird is a spiritual ideal, an allegory of a voyaging soul. It comes one day with its great spreading wings, flashing bright, writhing snakes of light, and then it vanishes, passing on to another place. Thunderbirds are the holy grandfathers.

Thunderbird is perched at the top of the world in the highest heaven. Beware of the power of thunderbird, the power of lightning bolts. Its eyes glow and from them twisting branch lightning stripes the sky and ricochets over the land. Thunderbird is the great thunder eagle and rainmaker, a majestic bird capable of creating devastating storms.

The bow and arrow were associated with the thunderbird totem – the bow representing the dome of the sky, the arrow the lightning. The arrow laid across the bow and ready to shoot made the shape of a bird, the arrowhead being its head and the bow its wings.

The thunderbird shaman was traditionally painted in black charcoal paint representing lightning-struck wood, with black signifying victory. On the ground was a gourd filled with water mixed with blue clay. Facing each direction, the shaman sipped from the gourd and using an eagle wing feather flicked the blue water into the air. The shaman then began chanting. Black clouds suddenly filled the sky, lightning flashed and the rains came.

With thunderbird as your supernatural ally, you travel on a journey to the mountain from where you can see the great distances of the holy earth. Thunderbird gives you the power to speak the everlasting truth. Someone with thunderbird as a spirit animal is not a person to make angry. Conversely, the thunderbird spirit can make people instantly happy. It is always wise to keep on good terms with the thunder beings.

THE SACRED CLOWN

In Native American cultures, once a person dreamed of the thunderbird, they became a sacred clown, a jester or contrarian. No one was allowed to touch this clown except other clowns. Variously called *heyoka, hohnuhk'e* or *koshairi* and many other names, these people were the thunderbird dreamers.

The sacred clown had a special relationship with lightning. This actually moves backward from the earth to the sky – and clowns were the backward people. They said that they were going east, but they went west; when they said yes it meant no; and in summertime they wore winter clothes. Contrarians did the opposite of what others did. They rode horses facing the tail, they danced backward, they cried at jokes, they laughed during solemn occasions and they said goodbye for hello. The actions of these comedians brought relief from the stresses of life.

There are times when being contrary is preferable to being conformist. Rely on the thunderbird to guide your instinct.

THUNDERBOLT: A HAMMER FROM ABOVE

Like the thunderbird, the Greek Olympian divinity Zeus was a ruler of the sky. He too was a hurler of crashing lightning bolts and the source of destruction. Fuloara was the Roman goddess of lightning, but how she used her powers is all but forgotten. In Norse mythology, Mjollnir is the axe or club responsible for lightning – Thor's spirit hammer. Thor was a god of the ancient Germanic pantheon adopted by the Vikings. The Aztec god Tlaloc sent down killing lightning bolts, and the Maya had a similar god named Chac. Watch a storm from a safe distance. Open your heart to its subversive energies.

STORK

NEW LIFE

The famous white stork, popularized in folktale and mythology, is found in Europe, Africa and Asia. These birds coast on thermal updrafts on long migratory journeys, using their wide wing-span to conserve energy. In fact, the Marabou stork has a wing-span rivaling that of the Andean condor, extending to an extraordinary 10½ft (3.2m).

The nest of the stork corresponds to the size of the bird; some have been measured at over 6ft (2m) in diameter and 10ft (3m) in depth. Storks are very faithful to their nests and will return to them year after year. This loyalty to the nest may be one reason why storks have long been associated with fertility and the delivery of babies in many cultures. Another explanation may be that storks arrive at their breeding grounds in Poland and Germany nine months after midsummer, this being the human gestation period. Storks were also considered models of conjugal bliss, as they were believed (incorrectly) to mate for life. Because of this association with fecundity, storks were encouraged to nest on houses and other buildings in the hope that they would bring fertility and prosperity.

Stork symbolizes new life. However, if this is your spirit animal the significance could be wider than an actual baby coming into your world. Metaphorically, a new life is a new beginning. This could be new ideas, blendings or combinations. New life could mean unseen spiritual powers unfolding like a chick from the egg. To lose one's old self (life) is to find another; this is an ancient spiritual law.

Storks are fabulous energy bringers and with stork as your spirit ally you will carry this same magic. Stork brings a certain exuberance, happiness and change, as well as strong connection to family and friends. As an omen it may be a gentle nudge to look after young children and the elderly. The spirit of stork is the spirit of life itself.

The Contemplation of Stork Power Exercise

The stork denotes longevity in the East and, in Taoism specifically, immortality. This exercise cannot promise such heights of attainment, but it can connect you to images of flight, openness and freedom, and hence be a good preparation for creative projects.

1. On a starry night, go outside to a quiet, open spot. Be centered and balanced and take a few deep breaths. Face the east. Lift your arms, and as you do so, imagine they are white stork wings. Do this several times while visualizing the stork in your mind's eye. Facing each of the four directions, in turn east, south, west and north, ask for the stork spirit to be with you. Call for the stork spirit from above and below. Ask the stork to make you a channel for new ideas, a flow of creative energy and fertility.
2. Stand facing the southwest but turn your head toward the southeast to locate the whitest star in that direction. Hold your left palm up as though you are catching the energy of that star. Imagine its beautiful white rays pouring into your hand. Now also stretch out your right arm toward the northwest with your palm down toward the earth. Feel the white star energy flowing through you and out of your right hand and from there to the earth.
3. When you feel sufficiently charged with stork energy, lower your arms and thank the stork for being there. Say goodbye and promise to act on any insight or new understanding you may receive.

THE FUSION OF SELVES

The stork held the key to the individual character of each human being. The word "ba" in ancient Egypt meant the aspect of the soul that made a person unique – the personality, which would survive death. This was represented pictorially as a human-headed saddle-bill stork flying from the tomb to reunite with the "ka," which was the essence given at birth. This act was a spiritual rebirth. Imagine your "ba" and "ka" fusing to create a new you, rooted in family yet supremely individual.

HUMMINGBIRD
THE SWEETNESS OF LIFE

The hummingbird flits by, then swoops and hovers in front of a hollyhock flower, inserting its long, needle-like proboscis inside the bloom to draw nectar, its wings a blur.

Some legends relate that the hummingbird is a piece of the sun come down to the earth to seek the love of a woman, and the hummingbird has been used as a love medicine since time immemorial. In other legends, the hummingbird brought the sacred tobacco plant to the earth. Some tribal people call the hummingbird the doctor bird of the shaman.

These fairy-like creatures are called hummingbirds because of the sound that their tiny, rapidly beating wings make as they hover. Hummingbirds are found in the far north of North America all the way down into South America and also range through the Caribbean islands. There are about 340 species of these vibrant birds with plumage of spectacular iridescent colors.

The bee hummingbird is the smallest bird in the bird tribe. Hummingbirds can fly forward and, uniquely, backward, as well as hover in mid-air. Each day they consume up to two-thirds of their body weight in nectar, the sweet fluid in flowers. They have the highest metabolism of any animal, with a heart rate as high as 1,250 beats per minute. At night, they can slow down their metabolism and enter a state known as torpor, where their heart rate drops to 50–200 beats per minute, reducing their need for food.

Not easily subdued, hummingbird spirit visits the sun daily in its constant struggle to bring light to the world. If hummingbird is your spirit animal, you will love travel and colorful places. You always can be counted on as a joyful companion. A hummingbird spirit totem will provide you with tireless energy and bring you the sweet nectar of happiness. It also gives you the ability to bring harmony and beauty to any situation; the hummingbird spirit does not hesitate to fight for its right to be.

THE HUMMINGBIRD GOD: HUITZILOPOCHTLI

The Aztec god Huitzilopochtli, Hummingbird of the Left, was so bright that no one could look at him. The great warrior souls had to hold their shields in front of their eyes and peer through arrow-struck holes to see him. Every so often these same warriors were allowed to return to earth as hummingbirds.

The wild amaranth plant was eaten by Mesoamerican natives over 8,000 years ago, and became domesticated. Statues of the hummingbird god were made of amaranth seeds and small portions were eaten during rituals devoted to Huitzilopochtli. The conquistadors were horrified at this practice and did everything in their power to eradicate the amaranth plant.

The hummingbird god's father was a ball of feathers, while his mother was Coatlicue, who also gave birth to the moon and stars. The tiny hummingbird had cosmic importance. Out of nowhere it appears, carrying a vast and complex freight of Aztec symbolism. Honor the hummingbird, for its truths are unfathomable.

A HUMMINGBIRD GARDEN

*If you live in a region where there are hummingbirds, attract them by putting out red feeders – they love the color red. Mix a syrup for them, made up of four parts of water to one part of cane sugar. This mixture equates to the average sucrose content of the flower that North American hummingbirds frequent, without being so sweet that clouds of insects will descend upon it. Flush the feeder with hot water between fillings, and clean with diluted bleach once a month. You might also plant a hummingbird garden, choosing the plants for color and nectar content (hummingbirds have little sense of smell). Try azaleas, begonias, honeysuckles, morning glory and bee balm (*Monarda*).*

LEOPARD

FEARLESS AND FAST

A leopard drinks from a pool of blue silver. The most elegantly striking animal in the cat family, she is secretive and elusive. Her green-gold eyes flash. She is an animal of immense power and daring. After the lion, tiger and jaguar, the leopard is the fourth largest cat. Relying on her muscular strength and on a much greater precision of attack than that of the tiger, she is a spotted mistress of camouflage, blending in to almost any environment.

In the classical world the leopard was an attribute of the god Dionysus (the Roman Bacchus) as creator-destroyer, and two leopards are often depicted pulling the chariot of Dionysus in art. The creature's spots were associated with the legendary many-eyed Argus.

Some cultures maintain that leopards can become completely invisible at will, and there are many legends of them as shape-shifters. There are said to be leopards with supernatural powers that transform into beautiful women and call men to their doom. Stories are told of certain witchdoctors who have the ability to change into leopards and other werecats. They wait in the night near deserted paths for their victims.

On a brighter note, this animal is clever, regal and graceful. The leopard has shorter legs than other large cats and can weigh up to 200 lb (90kg). Unlike lions and tigers, she can climb trees and poles. This means that she can fall on a prey from above. The leopard is crafty, and has an agile, lean, mean body with sharp claws and teeth.

There is great force in the loose and relaxed movement of the leopard, which can suddenly change into explosive fury. This big cat is greatly feared. Leopards are watchers that can change in an instant. This cat moves with awe-inspiring rapidity, striking with deadly accuracy. And this is the leopard's way. The leopard cannot change its spots, as the old maxim goes – but then it doesn't need to. In the realm of mind and intellect, or in a benignly competitive environment, none of this need be aggressive. Ride on a leopard, in your meditations, even if you choose not to *be* a leopard.

If leopard is your spirit animal, carry a leopardskin jasper as a talisman, preferably one found in nature, or any other stone marked like a leopard. This type of stone connects with decisiveness and leopard's warrior energy. Similar stones carried by shamans are said to give protection from aggression or danger. The stone can also be an aid in astral travel.

Leopard can teach you to see and hear things that others will miss. As your spirit collaborator she can help you assimilate knowledge quickly. Remember, speed follows on from silence – the calm before the attack. Meditations on leopard can bring you to focused stillness and compact, unstoppable power. The spirit of leopard can give you incredible alertness and an unhesitating response. She will teach you how to pounce.

THE MYSTICAL SNOW LEOPARD

The endangered snow leopard is nocturnal and is most active from dusk to dawn. These cats are built for mountain climbing, with short forelegs and long hind legs. Inhabiting the high mountains of Central Asia, they have a thick fur coat, gray with black rings. Their long furry tails may be well over a yard (1m) long – nearly as long as their bodies. They often curl up and use the tail as a sort of furry boa to keep warm.

Tales of the mystical snow leopard abound in China, India, Kazakhstan and Mongolia. In Tibet and Nepal there are legends of shaman lamas who shape-shift into snow leopards and travel long distances in this form. The great 11th-century master and poet-saint Milarepa was often observed in the guise of a snow leopard. In these ancient traditions, a shaman sitting on a sacred snow leopard pelt was propeled on a magic carpet ride to the upper spirits and the place of highest understanding – to the true opening of the wisdom gate. Conjure up your own snow leopard and travel to unimaginable realms.

UNICORN

EXQUISITE BEAUTY

There's an old adage similar to a Zen koan, or riddle: "The greatest blessing is a herd of unicorn." Perhaps, as with a koan, by unraveling its meaning one can reach *samadi*, a state of no mind – the last step to realization. Certainly, there is exquisite beauty in the possibility of enlightenment.

The unicorn looks like a horse, but with a long horn in the center of its forehead like the rhinoceros. In some depictions, the creature has the beard of a billy-goat, a lion's tail and cloven hooves. There are early cave paintings of unicorn-like creatures, and this mythological animal is represented in many cultures. The Greek physician Ctesus wrote in 400BC, "There are in India wild asses which are large as horses and sometimes even larger. Their bodies are white, their heads red and their eyes are a sapphire blue. On their forehead, they have a sharp white horn." He writes that the horn can be used as an antidote to deadly poisons and that those who drink from a cup made from the horn will never have epilepsy or any other kind of seizure.

Born of tenderness and loveliness, the unicorn can be tamed only by a virgin. If you catch a glimpse of this mysterious wanderer of the forest, be assured you have been many times blessed. It is an especially good omen to dream of the unicorn. Your troubles will soon be over – at least your financial or material troubles. The unicorn brings the "horn of plenty" or cornucopia into your life, associated with inexhaustible riches. With unicorn as your totem animal you will radiate good looks from the true beauty within.

The Austrian poet Rainer Maria Rilke (1875–1926), in one of his *Sonnets to Orpheus*, describes how the unicorn came into being from our very wish to believe in the implausible: the villagers fed the creature only with the possibility of its being, which made it sprout a horn on its head. Track down this beautiful poem and use it to summon unicorn into your own life.

THE CHINESE UNICORN

Along with the dragon, phoenix and tortoise, the unicorn is one of the four most important Chinese mythical animals. It appears in ages when there are munificent emperors and wise and knowing sages. The Chinese unicorn is stylized and colorful. The creature resembles a grand stag, which even in its fierceness is the epitome of benevolence and kindheartedness. The unicorn's beautiful voice is the sound of tiny tinkling bells and other delicate instruments. Its life-span is a thousand years.

Images of the Chinese unicorn surrounded by fire have a mysterious dragon quality and the unicorn was often referred to as the dragon horse. In one myth the emperor kept a unicorn at court when hearing disputes. It invariably gored the guilty party but never harmed an innocent person.

This fabulous creature is said to bring good fortune, a long and prosperous life, dutiful children, wisdom and goodwill. And reportedly, seeing a Chinese unicorn will immediately open the Third Eye.

DOLPHIN

SCHOOL OF JOY

Dolphins are marine mammals that breathe through a blowhole like whales, and they do, in fact, belong to the same order of animals. Dolphin skeletons reveal two small, rod-shaped pelvic bones thought to indicate the remains of hind legs – a sign that these were once land creatures. Male dolphins are known as bulls, females are called cows and a baby dolphin is referred to as a calf.

Dolphins are social animals and travel in groups, known as pods or schools. There is a long history of interaction between humans and dolphins; artefacts from ancient Greece and Rome depict boys riding dolphins while Greek myth is rich with tales of humans being saved from drowning by dolphins. Maori legends of New Zealand recount how their people were led to the "promised land" by dolphins. This bond continues today with many examples of dolphins interacting with humans both playfully and, more seriously, protecting swimmers from shark attack.

Many cultures associate the dolphin with divine or supernatural powers. According to Greek legend, Poseidon, the god of the sea, set the constellation of Delphinus, the dolphin, in the sky in gratitude for the sea creatures bringing him the nymph Amphitrite, with whom he fell in love and married. Dionysius, the god of wine and revelry, also honored the intelligence and co-operation of dolphins. He was set upon at sea by a band of pirates and transformed them into a pod of dolphins, charging them thereafter with the rescue of any distressed or drowning sailors.

In many parts of Asia dolphins are highly respected. In Vietnam a dead dolphin washed up on shore was mourned like a human death and the body buried. And amongst the native people of the Amazon, the river dolphin, known as the boto, was a great shape-shifter. It was believed at night he took the form of a handsome young man and could seduce innocent local girls, only to return to the river in the morning to become a dolphin once more. It was considered very bad luck to kill such a creature.

Marine biologists agree that the dolphin is highly intelligent although this is difficult for us to measure precisely. We know that the dolphin brain is large and complex, and structured differently to that of land mammals. Certainly, there is a light of intelligence in the eyes of a dolphin. This is the light of a great sage. The dolphin's sensitivity is beyond our ability to comprehend. Some people who work with dolphins say that the creatures can look into the soul of another. They seem to sympathize with people, a quality that has been recognized by humans over thousands of years. Dolphins embody the spirit of joyful intelligence and are willing to use it to help us.

With dolphin as your spirit animal guide, you will have a connection with the divine and experience delight in everything you see and do – it is the happiest of totems. You hold the source, the breath of life, and you spread love and happiness wherever you go. Your inner joy is contagious. You are indeed blessed and so is everyone who knows you.

INDRA'S NET: THE LINKING OF MINDS

The dolphin possesses a wide and deep planetary understanding, with knowledge of many spiritual seas, oceans, islands, lakes, rivers, gulfs and bays. One metaphor for the mind of the dolphin is the net of Indra, the Hindu king of the gods. Indra cast a great net over the globe – a net of consciousness that links all sentient life. Each living being is attached to this cognitive net like a sparkling jewel on a silken web. Each jewel has many facets, exceptional colors and various other qualities, with no two jewels alike, and each broadcasts a certain consciousness and frequency from its location on the net – these are the manifold jewels of Indra. They reflect off each other and shimmer with effervescent colors. Each jewel holds a piece of reality and every reality is different. Indra's net is the matrix, and these beautiful jewels, which are dolphins, emit an extra-high frequency. Every living thing reflects into the matrix, and each solitary jewel is connected to every other jewel linked in the infinite net of Indra.

FURTHER READING

Carson, D. *Crossing Into Medicine Country.* New York: Arcade Publishing, 2005.

Castaneda, C. *Journey to Ixtlan.* New York: Simon & Schuster, 1972.

Castaneda, C. *The Teachings of Don Juan: A Yaqui Way of Knowledge.* New York: Simon & Schuster, 1968.

Chevalier, J. and Gheerbrant, A. (J. Buchanan-Brown, Translator). *Dictionary of Symbols.* London: Penguin, 1996.

Harpster, H. T. *The Insect World.* New York: Viking Press, 1952.

Laubin, R. and Laubin, G. *Indian Dances of North America.* Norman: University of Oklahoma Press, 1989.

Roob, A. *Alchemy & Mysticism.* Köln: Taschen, 2006.

Stands In Timber, J. and Liberty, M. *Cheyenne Memories.* Lincoln: University of Nebraska Press, 1967

Storm, H. *Lightningbolt.* New York: Ballantine Books, 1994.

Storm, H. *Seven Arrows.* New York: Ballantine Books, 1973.

Voget, F. W. *The Shoshoni-Crow Sun Dance.* Norman: University of Oklahoma Press, 1984.

Waters, F. *Book of the Hopi.* New York: Penguin Books USA, 1963.

Williams, C. A. *Outlines of Chinese Symbolism & Art Motives.* New York: Dover Publications Inc, 1976.

Yellowtail, T. *Yellowtail Crow Medicine Man and Sun Dance Chief.* Norman: University of Oklahoma Press, 1991.

ORGANIZATIONS
FOR THE PROTECTION OF ANIMALS

If you feel inspired by your work with the animal spirit guides, you may feel you want to work directly for animal welfare. There are many groups offering different ways in which you can help, from sponsoring endangered animals to volunteering your services. Below is a list of just some of the many organizations you can contact.

The Africa Animal Protection Network

This organization aims at improving the care and well-being of animals on the African continent. It seeks to provide a co-ordinated strategy for dealing with issues such as poaching, the bush-meat trade and human–animal conflict.

For more information visit: www.africaanimal.org

Australian Koala Foundation

This charity funds research into koala populations in the wild, runs educational projects and aims to protect the koala's habitat.

For more information visit: www.savethekoala.com

The Born Free Foundation

The Born Free Foundation was inspired by the film of the same name describing the work of Joy Adamson amongst the lions of Kenya. The stars of the film, Bill Travers and Virginia McKenna, established the charity in 1984. Today, the organization is an international wildlife charity working to stop the suffering of wild animals and protect endangered species.

For more information visit: www.bornfree.org.uk or www.bornfreeusa.org

Endangered Species International

Endangered Species International is committed to saving endangered species and preserving wild places. The organization undertakes specific projects around the world, taking direct action, for example, to clean up after oil spills.

For more information visit: www.endangeredspeciesinternational.org

The Gorilla Organization

This organization was inspired by the work of Dian Fossey who lived among mountain gorillas for over twenty years and who did much to highlight the threats to their survival. The Gorilla Organization works internationally to save the last remaining gorillas in the wild.

For more information visit: www.gorillas.org

Whale and Dolphin Conservation Society

This is an international charity aimed at protecting whales, dolphins and their environments.

For more information visit: www.wdcs.org

World Wildlife Fund (WWF)

This international network was set up in 1961 and today is active in over 100 countries around the world. The WWF encourages people to adopt an endangered animal such as the giant panda, the orang-utan or the polar bear, by donating a sum of money each month.

For more information visit: www.wwf.org.uk

INDEX

N

O

P

Q

R

ACKNOWLEDGEMENTS

I am grateful for the mysterious way this book came to me and to the editors at DBP, Sandra Rigby and Bob Saxton. Thanks are also due to intellectual properties attorney M. J. Bogatin. Many thanks to Jon and Tracy, Jacqui and Jeff, Kelly and Mona, Greta and Joe, Jason and Jamie and, most especially, to Sara and Ken for their direct help. Also thanks due to my twin daughters, Maggie and Elizabeth, who are always an inspiration to me. And I can't forget the animals under my care and in my life just now: my three cats, Houdini, Fluffy and Raggy.